D1320299

The 247 Best Movie Scenes in Film History

The 247 Best Movie Scenes in Film History

*A Filmgoer's Guide to
Cigar Scenes, Car Chase Scenes,
Haircut Scenes, Whistling Scenes,
Dentist Scenes, Fluttering Drapes,
Funny Walks, Mirrors,
Name Mispronunciations,
Parking Meters,
Sagging Shoulders,
Steambaths,
and Numerous
Other Scenes
Long Noted
by
Aficionados.*

by
Sanford Levine

McFarland & Company, Inc., Publishers
Jefferson, North Carolina and London

British Library Cataloguing-in-Publication data are available

Library of Congress Cataloguing-in-Publication Data

Levine, Sanford, 1935–
   The 247 best movie scenes in film history / by Sanford Levine.
      p. cm.
   "A filmgoer's guide to cigar scenes, car chase scenes, haircut
scenes, whistling scenes, dentist scenes, fluttering drapes, funny
walks, mirrors, name mispronunciations, parking meters, sagging
shoulders, steambaths, and numerous other scenes long noted by
aficionados."
   Includes index.
   ISBN 0-89950-671-2 (lib. bdg. : 55# alk. paper) ∞
   1. Motion pictures–Plots, themes, etc. I. Title. II. Title:
Two hundred forty-seven best movie scenes in film history.
PN1997.8.L48   1992
791.43'75 – dc20   91-509531
                                                                   CIP

McFarland & Company, Inc., Publishers
  Box 611, Jefferson, North Carolina 28640

CONTENTS

B E S T S C E N E S

INTRODUCTION

B E S T S C E N E S

I suppose the idea for this book first came to me in the balcony of the old Symphony Theatre during a showing of *Citizen Kane*. On screen, Joseph Cotten was unsteadily relighting his cigar. Orson Welles had just fired him because he wouldn't write a good review of Dorothy Comingore's singing. When the scene was over, I got up and made my way to the lobby. Lately, I had begun to frequent a particular film just for a scene I particularly liked. I thought I was the only one doing this and was more than a little surprised to notice some people leaving with me. They caught up with me in the lobby: four men and a woman. One of them, a man in his mid-forties with a film buff's telltale pallor, asked me if I had come just for the cigar scene. When I replied that I had, the four men and a woman exchanged looks. The man with the movie pallor then introduced himself as Arnold Zellermeyer and suggested we have a little talk. Over a cherry lime rickey at a candy store with a real soda fountain, he explained to me what he and his colleagues had been up to. It wasn't a pretty story.

It all began when a few discerning cigar smokers, unable to satisfy their passion for Havana cigars legally, had begun to frequent films in which they suspected Havana cigars were being smoked. After a while, they started to recognize one another. This wasn't difficult since they seldom entered the theatre at the beginning of a film and rarely stayed more than a few minutes. Eventually they overcame their natural solitariness and began to speak to one another. Usually the conversation took the form of a tip on a film, where it was playing, the time the cigar scene went on.

It wasn't long before Zellermeyer discovered there were also movie fans who liked scenes in which there were no cigars. At a showing of *Paths of Glory*, he noticed a group of people walk out after Tim Carey killed the ant that Ralph Meeker said would still be around after they were shot. The following week he saw a group of people leaving the theatre after Joseph Cotten called Dr. Vinkle "Winkle." Over the next few months Zellermeyer saw groups of people walk out after marriage proposal scenes, button scenes, mirror scenes, laughing scenes, whistling scenes . . . even accounting scenes.

Being more sociable than most film fanatics, he gradually got to know the members of these disparate groups and it wasn't long before they formed an association. They called the association, D.O.A., an acronym for "Devotees of Film Art." Anticipating my question, Zellermeyer explained that the "F" remains silent in tribute to Edmond O'Brien, the star who was accidently poisoned in the film of the same name. At their bimonthly meetings, members of the D.O.A. soon began to discuss the content of the many different film scenes they had seen. The brand of a particular cigar smoked in a particular scene was haggled over, an actor checked for his whistling sensibility, a fluttering drape scene discussed for its symbolism – till eventually rules had to be introduced so the judging could be more exact.

As an example of what he was talking about, Zellermeyer read me the five criteria his own cigar group had established for determining the cigar rating of a film scene:

1. It must be a scene in which a fine cigar is smoked.

2. The cigar must be positively identified and its quality attested to by at least three members of the judging panel.

3. The cigar must be smoked with genuine pleasure.

4. The scene must not add anything to the plot of the film in which it appears.

5. No importance whatever should be attached to the length of the cigar scene, nor does a cigar have to be smoked or even appear on screen. (This rule, which may appear confusing since it conflicts with rules one, two, and three, will explain itself later.)

With criteria now firmly established, Zellermeyer's group was able to narrow down hundreds of exceptional scenes to a handful of such cigar excellence there remained only one thing left to do: let the world in on their accomplishment. Other groups, some of which had similiar sets of rules and some of which had no rules, had the same compulsion and began to choose the favorite scenes in their particular category.

Over a second cherry lime rickey, Zellermeyer handed me an envelope which contained a list of what he and his group considered the ten best cigar scenes in film history along with the names and addresses of the other member-groups of the D.O.A., in case I wanted to find out what scenes they considered worth listing. I was intrigued, after glancing briefly at the list, to see there was actually an ant scene fan club and a parking meter scene fan club in existence.

Before we parted, he gave me a brief example of how the judging of cigar scenes worked so I would not misundertand their selections. He suggested that I take a look again at rules 1 and 4. Zellermeyer said they would explain the absence of the 1953 film *Stalag 17* from the list. I could see what he meant. True, the scene in which William Holden lights a cigar to let Peter Graves know he knows he is the collaborator is a dramatic moment, but it violates rule 4 which states that a scene must not add anything to the plot. As for rule 1, it was violated by the subpar cigar Holden smoked.

It has been some time since that meeting with Zellermeyer. Over the next year, I managed to visit all the fan clubs who were members of the D.O.A., and some that weren't. The result is this book, a compilation of memorable film scenes, by category. The order in which the categories appear is alphabetical. The films within each category appear in no particular order. I believe it is the first time such a compilation of film scenes has been attempted. It is certainly the first time they have been made public.

Sanford Levine
Fall 1991

ACCOUNTANT

B E S T   S C E N E S

It's a Wonderful Life (1946). Probably the most woefully treated accountant in film history is Mr. Carter, the bank examiner from Elmira, New York, who had to spend Christmas Eve looking over the books of Jimmy Stewart's Savings and Loan. He not only never gets to examine the books, he has to stay late into the night waiting for them and then is forced into contributing a quarter to save Stewart from going to prison. Still, accountant scene fans persist in loving this scene if only because of the accountant sensibilities of the actor who played the role. (A check of both the screen credits, and the shooting script failed to turn up his name.) Though director Frank Capra insisted on calling him a bank examiner, Carter's accountant anima was so strong, no one objected when the scene was placed in this category. That it won its award easily, is already widely known in accountant scene fan circles.

═══════════

The Producers (1974). Within the profession they have been whispered about for decades – those legendary accountants whose sharp auditing methods have forced clients into farfetched claims of poverty. One C.P.A. from Pittsburgh is reported to have caught a general ledger posting inaccuracy that made his client, the owner of a chain of fur salons, aver he was so poor his kitchen table only had three legs. This was the yardstick accountants measured themselves by until Mel Brooks got into the accounting business. Brooks created Neil Bloom (Gene Wilder), the sharp-eyed accountant who discovered that Max Bialistock raised $62,000 for a flop that cost only $60,000 to produce. The discovery set a new standard for accountant scenes, earned this one its place in film history, and created a new legend. Gene Wilder will be talked about in the profession for years to come as the accountant who made Zero Mostel say he was so poor he had to wear a cardboard belt.

Cuba (1979). The two young American accountants in this almost forgotten Sean Connery film are still revered by accountant scene fans. Why? While doing the books for the Batista government general ledger they forgot about the revolution going on in the streets. When they finish the profit and loss statement one turns to the other and says, "Let's go out and see a little of Havana," a line many accountant scene fans rank with "Louis, I think this is the beginning of a beautiful friendship." Accountant scene fans do, however, fault the film for never mentioning if Castro appreciated getting a government with a P & L statement that balanced. This criticism may be explained by the fact that while one needn't be an accountant to be an accountant scene fan, many are.

Force of Evil (1948). In the accountant scene rule book, accountant appearance counts for a lot. The character, Mr. Bauer, Thomas Gomez's accountant in the numbers bank he ran, looked like an accountant. He wore glasses, he was bald, he blended into the scenery, and most importantly, when he put on his jacket, the back of it never touched his neck. In short, his accountant anima is so strong that accountant scene fans overlooked his breach of accountant confidentiality when he squealed on Gomez, and voted him a place in accountant history.

6

Midnight Run (1988). He was known as "the accountant," both by the mob he embezzled $15 million from and to the accountant scene fan club. Though Charles Grodin, a.k.a. "the Duke," did not have the "look" of an accountant, he did have the sensibilities of one. So attuned was he to the accountant persona that he immediately understood that when a ten-year-old-boy tells an embezzling accountant that he doesn't look like a criminal, he can always say, "I'm a white-collar criminal."

ANT

BEST SCENES

Paths of Glory (1958). In this classic anti–ant killing film from Stanley Kubrick, Ralph Meeker spots an ant crawling on the table in his makeshift jail cell. It is the evening before Meeker and Tim Carey are to be shot for cowardice. "You see that ant," Meeker says. "Tomorrow he'll be alive and we'll be dead." Carey looks at the ant, crushes it with his thumb, and says, "Now you got the edge on him." To many ant scene fans, it is the key scene in the film – a symbol of man's inhumanity to ants.

Some people even believe Meeker is as much to blame as Carey for the ant's death. They argue that if he hadn't revealed to Carey his deep-seated wish to change places with it, the ant might still be alive today. One gauge as to how much influence ant scene fans have in Hollywood is that neither Meeker nor Carey have worked in an ant film since.

The Naked Jungle (1957). Ant scent fans often point out that while the plot of this film revolved around a Brazilian ant army called *marabunta,* it had a much deeper subtext. This subtext revealed that it was really a film about antkind's desire to sail. Proof of this is the ants' final attack on Charlton Heston's plantation. When faced with a wide ditch of water surrounding the plantation, the army ants climbed a tree to cut off leaves and then dropped them to sailor ants waiting below. The sailor ants then

9

Ralph Meeker wanted to change places with an ant in the anti–ant killing film, *Paths of Glory* (1957) from Stanley Kubrick.

made leaf boats and sailed across the ditch. Ant scene auditors report that of the 7 trillion ant extras used in this film, nearly half knew how to sail leaves.

Them! (1954). Further proof that ants do not fare well on screen is this James Whitmore–Edmund Gwenn movie about mutant ants. At Gwenn's urging, the ant colonies are never given a chance to know that mankind meant them no harm as long as they behaved themselves. Instead, they are burned out of their desert colony and finally out of the storm drains of Los Angeles. An interesting footnote to the making of this film is that it was originally scheduled to be shot in Brooklyn, but the screenwriter and director didn't want the title of the film to be changed to "Dem."

No piece on ants in film should fail to mention the talents of Mel Blanc, an actor who knew his way around ant scenes. Blanc is the ant scene fan hero who created the ant-band sound many of us heard while watching cartoons as children. The sound can best be made by closing the mouth and going eh-eh-eh-eh through the nose.

If this doesn't describe what an ant band sounds like, the next best thing would be to hover near someone wearing a Walkman radio turned up loud. The sound you hear escaping from the earphones is very close to Mel Blanc's inspired version.

BALLOON

B E S T   S C E N E S

The Red Balloon (1957). If one can overlook some of the balloon slights in this film – mothers don't allow them in the house, schoolmasters don't allow them in schools, bus drivers don't allow them on buses, and little boys pelt them with rocks until they burst – one can understand why balloon scene fans have so much affection for the film.

Their favorite scene: Not the overly sentimental ending where balloons from all of Paris carry the little boy (Pascal) off, but the scene in which he is walking home from school in the rain. Since balloons aren't allowed on French buses, and Pascal didn't want his balloon to get wet, he asks an old gentleman if he and his balloon can take shelter under his umbrella. They walk home that way, from one umbrella to another. A charming scene and one that balloon scene fans never grow tired of watching.

An American Werewolf in London (1981). Henry Hull could never have done it. It took an American werewolf from N.Y.U. to pull off what admirers of this genre refer to as a classic balloon heist. Hiding naked behind a bush in a London park, David Naughton lures a little boy over so he could steal his balloons in order to wear them as underwear.

Though the scene lasts but a few seconds and has little to do with the plot, it won its place on the list because it resulted in a line

13

of dialogue that will be remembered as long as there are balloon enthusiasts left who speak the English language. It is delivered with just the right amount of matter-of-factness by a little English boy to his mother. "A naked American man stole my balloons."

The President's Analyst (1967). If you can accept a balloon being used to hold up a rock groupie's negligee so she can make love to James Coburn in a wheat field, you can accept this nomination for best balloon scene. There are some who might say that while a balloon holding up a negligee that is slowly rising into a cloudless blue sky is a lovely sight, it is not very realistic. Balloon scene admirers regard this point as irrelevant. They feel the scene deserves its place in film history because it is the only balloon scene on record in which a balloon is doing something practical.

The Third Man (1950). A temporary restraining order was lifted by the D.O.A. which allowed balloon scene fans to award this scene its place in balloon history. Here are the crucial elements of the scene upon which the decision was based: Trevor Howard, his sergeant and half the Austrian police force are waiting in the Vienna night to spring the trap on Orson Welles. There are footsteps, then a shadow appears on the far side of the square. It gets bigger and bigger as the man approaches. It is not Welles, but an old man selling balloons. He walks up to Trevor Howard and in the deepest bass voice yet to be heard in a balloon scene says, "Bahl-LOON? Bahl-LOON, mein Herr?" It turns out Howard doesn't want a balloon, but the sergeant buys one just to get rid of the balloon vendor.

That, essentially is the scene and those are the facts on which the decision to lift the restraining order were based. The two reasons the order was lifted were these: The first sighting of the balloon vendor was indeed a shadow, but it was a balloon shadow. Moreover, there was only one shadow, but there were 14 balloons, the second and strongest reason is that when the balloon man speaks he doesn't say, "sha-DOW," he says, "bahl-LOON!"

―――――――――――

There are a number of actors who have showed a partiality for balloons. Standing out among them are Peter Lorre, who had the good taste to buy one for his little victim in the German thriller, *M* (1931), and Danny Kaye, who in *Merry Andrew* (1958) preferred to wear his balloons inside his trousers.

BALLPOINT PEN

B E S T   S C E N E S

Breaking Away (1979). Whenever they are asked whether ballpoint pens are really important in the scheme of things, admirers of ballpoint pen scenes invariably cite this charmer directed by Peter Yates. The scene they always point to is the one in which Paul Dooley removes the fourteen ballpoint pens from his shirt pocket before making love to Barbara Barrie. They conclude that if Dooley hadn't removed those pens, Dennis Christopher would still be an only child.

Are ballpoint pens scenes important? Indeed! As important as procreation cry ballpoint pen enthusiasts across the country.

Seconds (1966). Ballpoint pen scene fans feel that most people who admired this John Frankenheimer film about medical science giving people a second life admired it for the wrong reasons. The star, John Randolph, does not want to look like Rock Hudson because he is going through male menopause. He wants to look like Rock Hudson because he realizes he can no longer do a crossword puzzle with a ballpoint pen.

The first hint is given during the agonizing commuter train ride when Randolph is seen holding the ballpoint in one hand and the crossword in the other but cannot put pen to paper. For anyone who did not pick up the message here, Frankenheimer rams it home when the pen Randolph is given so he can sign over

Paul Dooley removed fourteen ballpoint pens from his pocket before making love to Barbara Barrie in *Breaking Away* (1979).

his worldly possessions in order to look like Rock Hudson is a ballpoint.

———————————

Viva Zapata (1952). The inclusion of the scene in which Mexican dictator Porfirio Diaz circles Emiliano Zapata's name for asking that question about boundary markers is testimony to the stubbornness of ballpoint pen fans. Diaz couldn't possibly have been using a ballpoint. The facts supporting this argument are these: The film depicts events that took place in 1910. The ballpoint pen was not in use until about 1940. Ballpoint pen lawyers point out that this line of reasoning is full of holes. They admit that the events in the film took place in 1910, but contend that the film was actually made in 1952, twelve years after ballpoints were in use.

Ballpointers further contend that a ballpoint pen was used in the scene because neither Elia Kazan, the film's director, nor Marlon Brando, its star, were sticklers for historical pen accuracy. When asked to verify this theory, no one at 20th Century–Fox, the studio that made the film, was available for comment. Which leaves us with the question, "It's a great scene, but is it a great ballpoint pen scene?"

Rain Man (1988). Many ballpoint pen scene fans still believe that a large part of the credit for Dustin Hoffman's Oscar for his performance in this film should go to the ballpoint pens he always carried in his shirt pocket. This doesn't necessarily mean they consider ballpoint pens in the pocket to be a lucky talisman for an actor. Nor was it the reason they voted to include this film on the award list. It was Hoffman's ballpoint pen loyalty and his insistence on not leaving wherever he happened to be without them that really counted when the ballots were cast.

Nerds in Paradise (1987). The rumor that ballpoint pen fans passed up *Revenge of the Nerds* (1984) because they didn't like the nerd image projected by a plastic case filled with ballpoint pens is totally without substance. Ballpoint pen scene fans have consistently pointed out that ballpoint pens do not judge the character of the person in whose pocket they happen to find themselves. They are the first to admit there were a number of scenes in the earlier film in which ballpoints appear but feel that none were worthy of this award. With the selection of this nerd sequel, they hope the "nerd image" rumor will be finally laid to rest.

Ballpoint pen people feel the ballpoint pen scene chosen is not only worthy of an award, but is actually quite moving. It occurs in the final moments of the film, when a former campus jock (the guy the nerds saved when he was marooned on the island) is initiated into the nerd fraternity and presented with his plastic case containing 10 ballpoint pens. What endears the scene to ballpoint pen fans is that he really seems proud to receive it.

BIRD

How Green Was My Valley (1941). This simple tale of how a bird helped Roddy McDowall to walk again is often referred to as a bird classic. Walter Pidgeon sets the key scene up when he tells Roddy that he will walk again by spring. That's because Roddy had fallen through the ice to save his mother (Sara Algood) from drowning.

The scene that has bird scene enthusiasts all atwitter occurs when Roddy is lying in bed by an open window. At the door, his mother and sister (Maureen O'Hara) are watching. A bird flies by and lands on the windowsill. Roddy looks at the bird, then at his mother, and utters what many consider to be the most dramatic line of the film. In a voice filled with hope and bird love Roddy asks, "Spring?" After a few drinks, bird scene lovers, who do not usually make light of bird scenes, are likely to remark that if the bird hadn't landed on the windowsill Roddy would never have been able to make *Planet of the Apes*.

The Producers (1974). When Zero Mostel and Gene Wilder go to visit Kenneth Mars to tell him they want to produce "Springtime for Hitler," and are told by his landlady that, "He keeps boids. Dirty, disgusting, lice-ridden boids," the effect on bird scene fans in the audience is visible. They sense something is up and expect a payoff.

Happily, Mel Brooks, who directed this very funny film, doesn't allow Mars to let them down. After Mostel and Wilder tell him how much they love his play, Mars walks over to his rooftop pigeon coop, takes out one of the pigeons, kisses it and cries, "They're going to clear the Führer's name!"

Mon Oncle (1963). The great Jacques Tati's bird sensibilities were so highly developed that he knew instinctively that the canary in the courtyard below wouldn't sing unless the sun shined on it. Each morning before Tati left his apartment, he would fix his balcony window at a special angle so that the sun would reflect off it and on to the canary. This not only pleased the canary, who would begin to sing, but delighted bird scene lovers, who thought the scene so inventive they made its selection unanimous.

Broadway Danny Rose (1984). In great bird scenes, like great cigar scenes, birds need not appear on screen. They merely have to be talked about with feeling. Such is the case when the actor with the bird act complains to Woody Allen that a cat ate his lead act, "Peewee, the Bird." The fact that an actor was holding Peewee's empty bird cage during the scene may have weighed heavily in the voting. Like cigar scene fans, bird scene fans understand that in the making of an exhilarating bird scene, bird yearning counts a lot.

The Birds (1963). With so many bird scenes to choose from in this Alfred Hitchcock heartstopper about bird revenge, bird scene enthusiasts chose one that is actually funny. It occurs near the beginning of the film as Tippi Hedren is taking the two lovebirds to Rod Taylor. The cage is on the floor of her sports car on the passenger side. The birds are facing forward. As Hedren drives along the twisty coast highway, the camera, at floor level, shoots the two birds leaning in the direction of each turn. When the car turns left, the birds lean left. When the car turns right, the birds lean right. It is classic Hitchcock, who would have appreciated the choice.

To those who ask, "Why wasn't a more exciting scene chosen? The school children running down the hill being attacked by birds, or the birds flying down Rod Taylor's chimney?" the answer is quite simple. Many bird scene fans are also bird lovers and they don't like to award scenes that show birds in a bad light.

Dumbo (1941). One needn't be an avid bird scene fan to know that when one sees a crow smoking a cigar talking to an elephant in a tree, one can expect a bird scene that is considerably above the average. Walt Disney does not let us down. When the crows find Dumbo sleeping in a branch and sing, "Did you ever see an elephant fly," bird scene fans wonder if the delight they receive can be topped. They soon have their answer when the crows give Dumbo a magic feather, push him off the cliff and fly with him, singing, "I've seen everything when I've seen an elephant fly."

Though it isn't generally known, a claim was put in for this scene by cigar scene fans, but was quietly withdrawn when it became clear that it would be too difficult to judge the quality of an animated cigar.

The Ten Commandments (1956). The manner in which Yul Brynner announces the death of the Pharaoh (Cedric Hardwicke) still sends a frisson up the spine of bird scene fans. He steps in front of Hardwicke's deathbed and loftily proclaims, "The royal falcon has flown into the sun." So strong is the falcon image in Brynner's words that when they cut to an exterior shot of a sphinx in a cloudless, falconless sky, one can almost see a falcon. It was a sly move on the part of producer-director Cecil B. De Mille.

In fact, an unnamed source at Paramount, the studio which made this epic, recently confirmed what bird scene fans have suspected all along. De Mille did not use a falcon because he knew that the parting of the Red Sea was going to be an expensive scene to shoot and he had to economize where he could.

Visitors to the bird scene clubhouse in Oxnard, California, might be intrigued by the green parrot displayed on the mantlepiece. It is reported to be the stuffed remains of the parrot who flew around the deck of Douglas Fairbanks's ship in *Sinbad the Sailor* (1947) screeching, "Jamal, Jamal!" The parrot, a favorite of bird scene fans, was trying to tell Fairbanks that Jamal was really Walter Slezak before they reached the island of Derriabar. That the parrot is indeed the same bird as that used in the film was proven conclusively at a recent viewing of the film. In the final scene, when Slezak's eyes turn brilliant green after he drinks the poison he had intended for Fairbanks, the stuffed parrot was held next to the screen and was the same shade of green.

BRAIN TUMOR

B E S T   S C E N E S

Hannah and Her Sisters (1985). Brain tumor fans were taken completely by surprise when, of all the actors in this film, it was Woody Allen himself who gets the chance to play a character with a suspected brain tumor. There were many who felt that Mia Farrow would have been a better choice (all those kids without a mom). Lloyd Nolan would have looked infinitely better going under the CAT scan. But no, Allen kept the suspected tumor for himself, causing some brain tumor fans to openly accuse the film's writer/director of "brain tumor selfishness."

Though Allen gives himself some pretty good symptoms, such as loss of hearing in one ear and a spot on an X-ray, he left out suspicious smells, which didn't matter anyway since it turned out he didn't have a brain tumor after all. The small group of brain tumor fans, who felt it unfair that Allen lived with his "brain tumor" while Bette Davis died from hers, voted to keep this film off the list. Their sentiments kept the vote close, but did not change the final result.

Dark Victory (1939). Brain tumor fans point to this movie whenever they need to prove their theory that the rich have better brain tumor symptoms than the rest of us. Two of Bette Davis's more interesting symptoms were losing a bundle of money at

25

bridge (because of an inability to concentrate) and double vision when the horse she is riding is about to jump a fence.

Unhappily, even though Davis is married to a brain surgeon (George Brent), she never makes it out of her brain tumor scene alive. Her death is peaceful enough. Told she would know the end is near when she goes blind, she brightly waves Brent off to work, then calmly turns to her friend, Geraldine Fitzgerald, and asks to be lead back into the house. It's a moment brain tumor fans often point to when they talk about the character building qualities of brain tumors. Before Davis knew of her brain tumor, she was a spoiled socialite. Afterwards, she was a model wife. With the possible exception of Woody Allen movies, actors who learn they have brain tumors tend to act like that.

Stairway to Heaven (1946). Followers of brain tumor scenes consider this memorable and very original film to be the granddaddy of brain tumor movies. It stars David Niven as a World War II British pilot who jumps from his damaged plane without a parachute and survives. Niven's only injury, other than the fact that he has fallen love with Kim Hunter, is a brain tumor. The symptoms of his brain tumor are unique indeed. Niven smells fried onions before each visit by an 18th-century French courtier (Marius Goring), who can freeze people in time while he and Niven have their talks.

Goring explains to Niven that since he was supposed to die in the fall, Heaven wants him back. But because Niven has fallen in love during the time he was supposed to be dead, he will be allowed to appeal. Niven's doctor, played marvelously by Roger Livesy, thinks Niven is imagining all this because of his brain tumor. Livesy dies in a motorcycle accident the night he is supposed to operate on Niven. Instead of becoming Niven's brain surgeon, he becomes Niven's brainy lawyer. They all go up that wonderful staircase which literally goes to Heaven.

The stern Raymond Massey, the first American patriot killed

in the Revolutionary War, is the prosecutor. It is a particularly nice touch that the trial takes place during the operation. Niven wins his case, pulls through the operation, comes back down the staircase and is allowed to live out his full life span with Kim Hunter. A remarkable film, one that brain tumor fans admit to enjoying on levels which have nothing to do with the genre.

BUTTON

B E S T   S C E N E S

The Private Affairs of Bel Ami (1947).   Most button scene
enthusiasts consider this nearly forgotten film to contain not one
but two of the best button scenes in film history. When the actress
at George Sanders's knee begins to wind her hair around one of
his jacket buttons, the excitement can be felt from every button
scene fan in the audience. Heightening the effect is the lack of attention Sanders pays to her or what she is doing. When Sanders
suddenly gets up from the chair, taking a strand of her hair with
him, button scene fans have been known to literally jump from
their seats. An especially nice touch is how the camera lingers on
the woman's face to show the exquisite look of pain and pleasure
Sanders's button caused her. The knowledge that this strand of
hair would lead to another button scene keeps the attention of
button scene fans riveted on the button with the strand of hair
wound around it. There it remains until Angela Lansbury spots
the strand of hair on Sanders's button and utters the line everyone has been waiting for, "Oh, look, someone has wound their hair
around one of your buttons." Lansbury's words have recently
been immortalized in a needlepoint sampler which now hangs in
the Button Scene Hall of Fame.

It Happened One Night (1934). How the button scene in
this Frank Capra Academy Award winner got to appear in this

category is considered by some to be more interesting than the button quality of the scene itself. But scene fans now admit it was bequeathed to them by a former undershirt scene fan who knew that when Clark Gable unbuttoned his shirt to reveal he wore no undershirt, it would be the beginning of the end of the undershirt movie genre. Having been through all this with zippers, button scene fans understood the feeling and honored the bequest.

The contents of his will revealed that the late undershirt scene fan wanted Gable to win the award so the world would not forget the face of the man who was responsible for the almost total disappearance of undershirts in film. Because of all the commotion, the button quality of this scene, in which Gable shows Claudette Colbert in what order a man takes off his clothes through the use of buttons, was almost overlooked.

The Big Chill (1985). Merely the rumor that this scene was being considered for an award gave button scene enthusiasts a reputation for being morbid. True, the scene takes place in a funeral home, and yes, the object being buttoned is a corpse, and yes again, the mortician seems to be wearing red nail polish. To explain all this, button scene fans prefer to go over each point individually. First, they are always on the lookout for unusual button scene locales and what is more unusual than a button scene in a funeral home? Second, what else would be buttoned in a funeral home but the clothes on a corpse? Finally, they resent any untoward suggestions deriving from the fact they like a scene in which a mortician wears red nail polish, pointing out the obvious – the mortician was a woman.

Father of the Bride (1950). Isn't it odd how buttons bring out the worst in wives? Joan Bennett is the sweetest of women all through this delightful comedy of manners, but when faced with a button scene she suddenly develops a sharp tongue. It happens while Spencer Tracy is trying on his old cutaway. Tracy, who hasn't worn his tails in twenty years, does a boffo job of proving he can still fit into them by managing to button every button of his very tight vest. He tops this off with the jacket, which he can barely get his arms into. Tracy manages to button its one button only after finding a posture that makes him look like a cross between Dr. Frankenstein's humpbacked servant and Walter Matthau.

So what is Bennett's reaction to all this when Tracy calls her in to view the result of his efforts? She takes one look at the button on Tracy's jacket and delivers what must be one of the meanest button lines in recent screen memory, "If that button gets away, it's going to put out someone's eye!"

CAR CHASE

B E S T S C E N E S

Bullitt (1968). At the opening of the monthly meeting of the car chase scene fan club, the chancelor raps his gavel and asks the members, "Why are there hills in San Francisco?"

"So there can be great car chase scenes!" the members roar back.

The basis for this ritual is the classic car chase scene in this taut thriller. When Steve McQueen suddenly guns his sports car around the block and winds up tailing the killers who were tailing him, car chase fans can feel their antennae go up. When the driver of the car McQueen is tailing spots him in the rearview mirror and buckles his seat belt, and the killer beside him does the same, car chase fans take out their portable seat belts and buckle up, too. (No true car chase fan ever goes to see this film without one.)

The actual chase is not only wonderfully orchestrated and photographed, it develops a definite rhythm each time one of the cars reaches the crest of a hill, leaves the ground and thumps back to earth. The chase picks up even more speed and tension as it makes its way out onto the freeway where McQueen has to submit to a shotgun blast before the killers meet their fiery end by ramming into a gas truck.

One group of car chase scene arithmeticians has been trying to work out how many minutes the chase was on screen, but are unable to agree on when the chase actually begins. A second

Why are there hills in San Francisco? So there can be great car chase scenes! *Bullitt* **(1968).**

group has been attempting to work out how many miles were covered in the chase and whether or not one or both cars should have run out of gas. That both reports are many years overdue does not diminish the brilliance of this chase, which to date has not been topped.

———————

Foul Play (1978). When Gilbert and Sullivan wrote *The Mikado* in 1885, neither one had a car chase in mind. But don't tell that to car chase scene fans who consider the music to this operetta to be the perfect background score for one. The car chase in the film is a witty parody of the one in *Bullitt*. It, too, takes place in San Francisco. The action begins when Chevy Chase and Goldie Hawn commandeer a limousine so they can get to the opera to prevent the assassination of the Pope, who is seeing *The Mikado*.

34

To a car chase fan, the reasons for the chase don't matter, it just has to be a good one. This one is, with all the necessary ingredients – intersection running, sidewalk hopping, sudden turns and fender bending – that one would expect. There's even an unexpected bonus. There is an elderly Japanese couple in the rear of the limousine who do not speak English. They huddle in the back, not knowing what is happening until Chase tries to tell them he is a policeman and Hawn mentions "Kojak." This they understand and enjoy the rest of the ride, a nice touch and one that garnered the scene enough votes to put it on the list.

The French Connection (1971). Probably the least desirable place in the world to shoot a car chase is New York City. But a car chasing a subway train is another matter altogether. For this type of chase to work, the subway has to be above ground. No problem. New York City has plenty of those. Also, Gene Hackman has to commandeer a car. No problem. Hackman steps in front of a speeding car and gets the driver to give it to him by saying, "Police emergency. I need your car." Even usually serious car chase fans never fail to be amused when the driver asks Hackman (who has already begun to speed away), "Hey, when am I going to get it back?" Better he should never have asked.

Chasing a subway train speeding 30 feet over your head involves a lot of looking up. Hackman rams the poor fellow's car into a truck, another car, a few steel girders, and nearly hits a mother pushing a baby carriage. But he keeps up with the train and pays back the drug smuggler who tried to kill him by killing him. To those who think subway trains are easy to follow because they can't leave the tracks, car chase scene fans simply repeat what Hackman says when asked the same question, "Try chasing one!"

It's a Mad, Mad, Mad, Mad World (1963). When asked what movie contains a car chase that has cars, trucks, planes, fire-

35

works, and a mother-in-law, lasts for the entire movie, and is carefully mapped and followed by a long-suffering policeman who is trying to settle a domestic dispute between his wife and daughter, very few film fans would fail to name this movie. Car chase scene fans feel no other reason for their selection is necessary and rest their case.

CARD

The Cincinnati Kid (1965). A card scene fan following Steve McQueen's poker odyssey along the three river towns might feel like a kid in a candy store. There are so many memorable card games that choosing the best one is as difficult as trying to fill an inside straight. The one finally chosen is a poker hand early in the film. Rip Torn and Edward G. Robinson are playing a game of five card stud, head to head. McQueen, the main character, isn't even present. The last card has just been dealt. Torn bets $2,000. He shows no pair and no picture card. Robinson, who also shows no pair and no picture card, calls and raises $2,000. Torn calls the raise. He has jack high, no pair. Robinson wins the hand with queen high, no pair.

Not a particularly masterfully played hand, but one that won card scene fans over because of Robinson's devastating reply to Torn when he asks him how he knew he only had a jack as his hole card. "Son," Robinson says, "all you pay is the looking price. Lessons are extra."

Captain Horatio Hornblower (1951). Though few card scene fans even know how to play whist, many know a great whist scene when they see one. This is a great one and Gregory Peck's portrayal of an English sea captain with a passion for cards is flawless. When he invites his officers to his quarters for a rubber of whist, not knowing whether the enemy Spanish ship *Natividad* will sail around the point or snug down for the night, card game sceners are ashiver with anticipation. If the *Natividad* snugs down for the night, they know they will see a rubber of whist completed. It if spots Peck's ship, they will see whist players blown out of the water doing what they love best – playing whist. As the *Natividad* makes its final tack, Peck even takes the time to lecture one of his officers on the correct card to play.

The fact that Peck risks his life and those of his men betting the Spanish ship will snug down for the night so he could finish the rubber adds much to the tension and eventual pleasure of this scene. The scene is also proof that the Napoleonic War of 1812 could produce a first-class game of cards.

***

Alice in Wonderland (1951). Always in need of an extra hand, card scene fans have given this winning entry from Walt Disney a warm welcome. One reason it was allowed to sit down at the table with the big boys may be that card scene fans have always secretly considered cards as soldiers and hands as battles. So when an army of playing cards marches across the screen to herald the entrance of the Queen of Hearts, card scene fans are more delighted than surprised. Favorite scene: When the card army arranged itself into a deck of cards. Best song: "They're going to lose their heads; they painted the roses red." Funniest scene: When the cards arrange themselves as wickets in the croquet game between Alice and the Queen of Hearts.

***

The Foxes of Harrow (1947). Card scene fans who had been waiting for someone to cry, "Innkeeper, pen and pencil," at a dramatic point in a game of cards are rewarded in this scene in which Rex Harrison wins a plantation from a loudmouthed card player with a German accent. That alone would be enough to put it in the awards category, but there is more. We are treated to a streak of card player luck that is rare in films. Harrison sits down to a game of chemin-de-fer as a pauper, with nothing more than his lucky tie pin, and gets up a member of the landowner gentry.

If that isn't enough to fill an inside straight, we get to see the loudmouthed card player turn out to be a poor loser, insult Harrison, and get killed in a duel. The game is so superbly orchestrated and the loudmouthed cardplayer enough of a boor, few film fans mind when he gets shot.

The Odd Couple (1968). No collection of great card scenes could ever be complete without a weekly card game and no one knows how to capture the feel of a weekly game better than Neil Simon. Simon doesn't even make us wait long. He comes across with one in the opening scene of this very funny film. It has the right amount of card players, the right amount of smoke and the right amount of six-week-old potato chips.

From the moment Vinnie (the winner who always had to be home by twelve) asks what time it is and is told, "You're winning $95, that's what time it is," card scene fans know they are in the hands of someone who probably hasn't missed his Thursday night poker game in 15 years. Walter Matthau's eloquent rationale for why he plays poker touched the heart of every card scene fan present at the final vote. Matthau explained that he plays cards because he needs the money. He always loses. Which is why he needs the money.

It would be difficult to list all the actors who looked as if they were born holding a deck of cards, but three that most often top the list are Judy Holiday, for beating Broderick Crawford every time at gin in *Born Yesterday* (1950), Frank Sinatra for bluffing Dean Martin out of pot in *Some Came Running* (1959), and Dean Martin in the same film for taking it with such good grace.

CAT

B E S T   S C E N E S

The Wrong Box (1967). When Peter Sellers uses a kitten as a blotter in his role as the seedy Dr. Pratt, a roar of disapproval went up from cat lovers. Cat scene lovers, on the other hand, voted it as one of the the best cat scenes in film history. The same opposite reactions occurred when Peter Cook accidently sat on one of the many cats in Sellers's office. One needn't be a great genius to see that a cat lover is not necessarily a cat scene lover nor a cat scene lover a cat lover. Perhaps it was to appease the former group that Sellers informs the kitten he had used as a blotter that, "I was not always as you see me now."

Cinderella (1949). Cat lovers again cried foul. Lucifer, Walt Disney's cat villain in this animated fairy tale, would certainly have stopped Jacques and Gus (Cinderella's two mice friends) from delivering the key to her had it not been for Bruno, the dog. To cat scene lovers it didn't matter a whit that the key allowed Cinderella to unlock the door, try on the glass slipper and marry the Prince. Nowhere in the Cat Scene Manual does it say that great cat performances need to be burdened with plot considerations or that cats have to be treated with kid gloves. Cat lovers, on the other hand, felt that it was grossly unfair for Disney to bring in a dog to stop Lucifer from keeping Cinderella from being rescued by the two mice.

So high did feelings run among the cat lover clique in the cat scene lover clubhouse that they vowed to get even. They made good that vow six years later. The two Siamese cats in Disney's *Lady and the Tramp* (1955) were denied an award they justly deserved and were consigned to cat scene oblivion.

─────────────

The Invisible Man (1937). Another scene that cat scene lovers love and cat lovers don't occurs in the film starring Claude Rains in the title role. The award-winning scene comes towards the end of the film while the police are protecting Dr. Kemp from Rains. Kemp is Rains's former assistant and Rains has promised to kill him for calling the police on him. To make sure they can detect the invisible Rains, the police first put earth on top of the wall surrounding the house. That way they will see the earth move if Rains attempts to climb over. Then, they arm themselves with spritzers filled with paint. The idea is that if Rains does get on the grounds, one spritz and they'll see him. The plan backfires when a cat leaps onto the wall. A clump of dirt falls on one of the policemen, who then sprays the poor cat full of paint. The spritzer plan may not have caught Rains, but it did result in a memorable cat scene.

─────────────

The Incredible Shrinking Man (1957). In this film about cat revenge, cats get even for one of their number's getting sprayed with paint in *The Invisible Man* (1937). Cat lovers, however, were not mollified. They feel that the film portrayed cats as ungrateful animals who will eat their masters the moment they shrink. They cite the scene when the cat tries to do just that after discovering that her master had dropped to the size of a mouse and was living in his daughter's doll house. Cat scene lovers would not comment on this, but were reported to be amused when a group of cat lovers petitioned the government to make doll houses cat proof.

Breakfast at Tiffany's (1961). With the selection of this Audrey Hepburn film, cat scene lovers began to realize that cats do not fare well in films. Hepburn not only doesn't give her cat a name (referring to it simply as "Cat"), she tosses it from a taxi in the middle of a rainstorm. When she finally decides to keep it and goes looking for it in the rain, the audience knows that Hepburn is fully capable of caring for someone, even if it is only a cat. It is a dramatic moment that weighed heavily in the vote — making it clear that to a cat scene lover, cats as a catalyst count for a lot.

The Third Man (1950). A cat is the first to know that Harry Lime (Orson Welles) is alive. When it scoots out of Valli's apartment and down the deserted Vienna street, cat scene fans in the audience have a hard time restraining themselves from egging it on. By the time the cat stops at a doorway and begins to lick someone's well-shined shoes, everyone in the audience knows that Harry Lime isn't dead. It's not that difficult to figure out since we already know that Harry Lime is the only person the cat likes. A shaft of light from the window, a zither crescendo, and Welles's insolent smile when the light hits his face top off a cat scene worth remembering.

Actors who have shown a particular sensitivity to cats include all the heads of S.P.E.C.T.R.E. in all the James Bond films and Kim Novak, who used her cat, Piwacket, to cast a spell on Jimmy Stewart in *Bell, Book, and Candle* (1958). What won cat scene lovers over was how good a sport Novak was when she lost Piwacket's affections because she fell in love with Stewart.

43

CEMETERY

B E S T   S C E N E S

The Third Man (1950). Cemetery scene fans have a special fondness for movies in which the final scene is set in a cemetery. So when Joseph Cotten gets out of Trevor Howard's jeep to wait for Alida Valli outside that Viennese cemetery, they are all rooting for her to forgive him for shooting Harry Lime. As she walks towards Cotten, the zither crescendo gives them reason to believe she will. But Valli walks past him. Worse, she doesn't look at him. One of the great movie endings, but romantically disappointing. It should be noted that cemetery scene fans find the rumor that Valli could forgive Cotten for killing Lime, but not for getting Vinkle's name wrong, to be in very bad taste.

The Good, the Bad and the Ugly (1967). Cemetery scene delicacy is not one of Clint Eastwood's strong points. In the final cemetery scene of this Sergio Leone release, he shoots Lee Van Cleef and strings up Eli Wallach so he has to balance on a wooden grave marker or hand. Then Eastwood rides off to leave him. When Wallach protests, Eastwood, in what must be the best feat of cemetery scene marksmanship in screen history, casually takes out his rifle and shoots down the rope. In a separate ballot, cemetery scene fans voted this the best cemetery scene in a spaghetti western, which to some movie fans is like being voted the best second baseman in Bulgaria.

Mr. Hulot's Holiday (1954). Not even a cemetery could restrain the irrepressible Jacques Tati. In cemetery scene circles, the cemetery scene he created in this French import is considered a masterpiece of timing and wit. To work as it did, three crucial elements had to fall into place: Tati's spare tire had to roll into the wet leaves; he had to pick it up at the exact moment a funeral party arrives at the cemetery; the funeral party had to mistake the leaf-covered tire for a wreath and Tati for a mourner. The rest was easy. Tati was too sweet-natured to refuse their invitation to join them at graveside and too polite to tell them not to nail his spare tire into the tree.

One group of cemetery scene fans were so taken with this scene they plan to travel to Jacques Tati's gravesite to recreate it. Other than finding an automobile tire thin enough to be mistaken for a funeral wreath when covered with wet leaves, they foresee no difficulty.

Freud (1962). With the selection of this now almost forgotten John Huston film about a Viennese cemetery's contribution to psychiatry, cemetery scene fans seem to be saying that cemeteries are not a good place to resolve an Oedipus complex. Montgomery Clift found this to be true when Freud, the character he portrayed, fainted at the cemetery gates during a visit to his father's grave. For Freud, it was a breakthrough – the formulation of one of his most important theories. For cemetery scene fans it was simply a good cemetery scene, better than most and certainly deserving of this mention.

The Wrong Box (1969). For cemetery scene fans whose tastes for funerals run to undertakers in top hats draped with crepe, this English import has two sets of undertakers in top hats draped with crepe. For those who enjoy a high speed chase with horse-drawn hearses, a switch of caskets, and a knockdown brawl between the two "corpses," this very funny film obliges once again. Add to all this a game cast that refused to be buffaloed into solemnity at funerals – Dudley Moore, Fred Cook, Ralph Richardson, John Mills, and Michael Caine, to name a few – and one has what one cemetery scene fan, who rates them the old-fashioned way, calls a four-star cemetery scene.

The African Queen (1951). Perhaps the quickest and least sentimental funeral in film history is the one given to Robert Morley, who didn't quite make it through the first fifteen minutes of the movie alive. Humphrey Bogart's explanation of the hasty burial is also lacking in tender feelings. He tells Katharine Hepburn (Morley's sister), "What with the climate and all, the quicker we get him in the ground the better." Sentimentality aside, cemetery scene fans have a particular warm spot for this very brief funeral because cemetery scenes shot in Africa are rare. Best lines: Bogart's delicately phrased response when Hepburn tells him that Morley is dead, "Aw, ain't that awful."

Frankenstein (1931). A cemetery scene collection without a Frankenstein film would be like a werewolf movie without a full moon. Cemetery scene fans may have placed this one last on their list in order to cap their category off with a classic, but James Whale, the film's director, opened with his. It's a cemetery scene with all the necessary ingredients: fog, and a gravedigger with the right touch of nonchalance. This plays wonderfully against the tension of Colin Clive (Herr Frankenstein) and his servant Fritz, who wait behind the gate for the gravedigger to finish filling in the grave.

An especially nice touch is the exaggerated sound of the earth hitting the wooden casket. Cemetery scene fan sound experts report that this may be the loudest instance of earth hitting a wooden casket in film history. Best moment: As Clive and Fritz are digging up the casket, Clive sort of hugs it, exclaiming with great excitement: "He's just resting, waiting for a new life to come!"

Western cemetery scene fans felt a special honor should go to Ward Bond. Bond, who could sing "Shall We Gather at the River" with the best of them, was paid this mark of respect for finding time to attend nearly every western funeral ever filmed.

CIGAR

B E S T S C E N E S

Doctor Zhivago (1965). That is indeed a Havana cigar butt Sir Ralph Richardson is waving around with such excitement. It has been identified by the required number of experts as the partially-smoked remains of a Por Larranaga Corona Claro. Though the scene does not last for more than a minute, Richardson won a Kipling* for the true feeling he puts into his line, "I am about to smoke the last half of the last English cigar in Moscow." His words struck a particularly responsive chord in the breast of every cigar scene fan in the audience. [*Cigar scene fans have only recently introduced this award, which goes to the actor who performs in the winning scene. It is called a "Kipling," after the English writer, Rudyard Kipling, whose poem "Bethrothed" compares the virtues of cigars to those of women.]

Lifeboat (1944). This film has earned its place on the list if only for the extraordinary length of time a cigar is seen on camera. The manner in which Henry Hull nurses his solitary Bolívar Corona Gigante through storm, poker game, drought and, finally, the murder of Walter Slezak, is a lesson in platonic cigar love from which many cigar smokers could benefit. It is only natural that a film in which cigar lifeboat etiquette is raised to such heights should be the one which superficially appears to violate rule 5 in the Cigar Scene Manual. Rule 5 refers to the

49

Simon Ward as Winston Churchill smoking his first cigar in _Young Winston_ (1972).

unimportance of cigar scene length. Most dramatic scene: Not the sly manner in which Walter Slezak causes the watery demise of William Bendix, but Hull's unfortunate discovery that the box of Havanas he has rescued from the sinking ship contains only one cigar.

━━━━━━━━━

_P.J._ (1968). To a cigar scene fan, Raymond Burr will forever be the granddaddy of cigar misers. With an entire humidor filled with expensive Cuban cigars, Burr kept a special section for butts. Though Zellermeyer reports that he was privately shocked at the sight of all those half-smoked Havanas, he confesses that it was the look in Burr's eyes as he fondles his cigar-butt treasure which won this scene a place on the awards list and exonerated him of the murder of the beautiful Gayle Hunnicut.

Witness for the Prosecution (1958). Who but the most phlegmatic of cigar smokers would fail to feel a frisson of terror watching Elsa Lanchester trying to ferret out Charles Laughton's hidden cigar. Laughton's ingenious ability to keep his cigar lit in the face of Lanchester's determination to deny him this pleasure has won him his well-deserved Kipling. Laughton's deft cigar frisk of the solicitor and his willingness to listen to the boring details of the case are the main charms of this film.

One cigar scene enthusiast reports that he learned the trick of keeping his cigar-hating third wife ignorant of his cigar habit from Laughton's clever maneuvering to always have a third party present whenever he wished to enjoy a cigar. When discovered, one could always rely on the visitor to claim ownership. Film historians may be interested to learn that Laughton was the first actor to use a cigar "beard" on screen.

Citizen Kane (1941). This classic film actually contains two memorable cigar scenes and Joseph Cotten, among all the great cigar-smoking actors in Hollywood, is the only one to pull off a "double claro," winning two Kiplings for a single performance. The first award is for his sensitive relighting of his Partagas Lusitania after Welles discovers him drunk over his typewriter. There were some in the selection committee who felt this first Kipling was a sentimental choice. After all, wasn't he fired by Welles after he relights it? And wasn't it his love of cigars that kept him a bachelor during the film?

Cotten's second Kipling was more unanimous. His portrayal of an old man yearning for a cigar has yet to be equalled on the silver screen. He literally has cigar scene fans at the edge of their seats when he tries to enlist a young reporter to sneak a "see-gar" into his old-age home. "You don't happen to have a good see-gar on you?" he asks. "I have a young physician who thinks I shouldn't smoke." Thrilling words, topped only by Cotten's final plea. "You won't forget those see-gars, will you? Make 'em look like toothpaste or something." If there is a more moving moment in cigar film history, I haven't seen it.

The only flaw in the film is that Welles, a cigar smoker himself, never allows us to see if the young reporter kept his promise.

Charlie Bubbles (1968). Cigar scene fans especially like this film if only for the infinite variety of places in which Albert Finney smokes a cigar. Finney smokes what have been definitively identified as Montecristo #1's while getting crème brûlée pushed into his face; while getting drunk in a pool hall; while watching a soccer game; while watching television monitors in his Georgian home; while driving his Rolls Royce; and, in what is Zellermeyer's favorite scene of all, while drying Colin Blakely's trousers in the men's room at Hyde Park.

The Formula (1980). Proof that a memorable cigar scene need not contain smoke comes by way of the inclusion of this film about cigar theft. When Detective Rizzo invades the humidor of George C. Scott's murdered friend, practically everyone in the audience thinks him to be a ghoul. Not cigar scene fans, however, who not only rooted for Rizzo, but have yet to forgive Scott for the mean-spirited manner in which he makes Rizzo put the cigars back in the humidor. Though the cigars Rizzo tried to filch were not of the finest quality, there were few dissenting voices raised when this scene was discussed. The reason for this apparent violation of rule 1 is that when Kiplings are handed out, cigar yearning counts a lot.

The Seventh Veil (1945). Every cigar smoker will appreciate the wily manner in which James Mason attempts to get the no-good artist to paint Ann Todd's portrait. He offers him a delectable supper and an impeccable cigar. The sight of James Mason and the artist sitting in that drawing room is enough to make any serious cigar scene fan levitate from his theatre seat. While of no real importance to the film, and lasting all of 27 seconds, the scene is so drenched in pungent cigar atmosphere that it breezed into a place on this list.

———————

The Maltese Falcon (1941). Many admirers of this classic cigar whodunit hold the mistaken notion that Sydney Greenstreet doctored Humphrey Bogart's drink so Elisha Cook would have an easier time of kicking him in the ribs when he blacked out. This was not the case. New evidence from Greenstreet's secret cigar diary supports Zellermeyer's long held theory that Bogart actually fainted with pleasure from the H. Upmann Double Corona offered him by the Fat Man.

Greenstreet's cigar persona is so profound that many of his fans are still not certain whether he was smoking one when he proposed to Elsa Lanchester in *Three Strangers* (1946). So beautifully did he portray a panic-stricken cigar smoker in *Maltese Falcon* that he has long since been forgiven for smoking cigarettes in *The Mask of Dimitrios* (1944).

———————

There are many other fine actors who knew their way around a fine cigar, and no piece on the pleasures of cigar scenes would be complete without giving them a mention. The list is only partial, but is dedicated to all screen actors who have shown the proper cigar delicacy in their roles: Charles Coburn for the Rey Del Mondo Lonesdales he smoked in *The Paradine Case* (1948); John Huston for his masterful portrayal of a cigar-smoking cardinal in *The Cardinal* (1963); Lee J. Cobb for *On the Waterfront*

(1954); Edward G. Robinson for *Key Largo* (1948); Eugene Palette for the patient manner in which he smoked his Montecristo #2's in *100 Men and a Girl* (1937); and Simon Ward for his sensitive recreation of Winston Churchill smoking his first cigar in *Young Winston* (1972). Finally, a special salute to Sean Connery, who in the film *Cuba* (1979), takes a tantalizing 41-second walk through a factory in which Cuban cigars are being made.

CIGARETTE CASE

B E S T   S C E N E S

Now, Voyager (1941). Everyone talked about the way Paul Henreid lit two cigarettes at a time and placed one in the lips of Bette Davis, but it took a sharp-eyed group of cigarette case fans to notice the nifty cigarette case he removed them from. The result of this observation opened up the possibility that Henreid's cigarette case may have been packed too full and he took out the extra cigarette to relieve the overcrowding, not to be nice to Miss Davis. It also changes the entire meaning of the last line of this film. The "stars" Davis refers to when she says, "Let us not ask for the moon, when we have the stars," may have been a reference to the intricate design on Henreid's cigarette case.

The Private Affairs of Bel Ami (1947). To show George Sanders how much she loves him, Angela Lansbury secretly measures his cigarette case so she can fit a photograph of herself inside it. During that now famous ride in a coach, she asks him for his cigarette case and places her photo inside it, delivering the line that is so loved by cigarette case fans, "I can measure the dimensions of this cigarette case, but who can measure the dimensions of your heart." Sanders, who must have realized this would become a classic cigarette case scene, responded with an equally immortal line, "I could be happy with you, Clothilde."

A New Leaf (1971). In this very funny film about the value and price of cigarette cases, Walter Matthau is no hero to cigarette case fans. Yes, he gives his cigarette case to his smarmy lawyer to satisfy a $550 debt, but he does it at the very beginning of the movie, making it a certainty the cigarette case will not be seen again. Even the fact that this is a film starring and directed by Elaine May is not enough to dissuade cigarette case fans from leaving the theatre after this scene is over.

Seven Days in May (1964). Had it not been for Edmund O'Brien's cigarette case, Burt Lancaster might have become the first Army general to overthrow the American government. Cigarette case enthusiasts, unused to seeing cigarette case scenes play such an important role in a film, flock in droves to this film about the value of keeping important documents in cigarette cases. The scene they come for is the one in which the Spanish soldier finds O'Brien's cigarette case in the plane wreckage. It was the same case given to him by the president of the United States. O'Brien had the foresight to put the signed confession he had obtained from an admiral into that very cigarette case. The case, and the evidence needed to foil the plot against the president, survived the crash. Unfortunately, O'Brien, now fully recovered from having been murdered in *D.O.A.*, did not.

CLOCK

B E S T S C E N E S

The Stranger (1946). When Orson Welles doesn't like a character he is playing, he certainly knows how to do him in. The beneficiaries of this sentiment are clock scene fans who are treated to what may be the first "clock murder" in film history. Welles, who starred in and directed this film, plays a Nazi with a mania for clocks. It is the final scene, set in the old clock tower, which strikes the fancy of clock scene fans.

By the time of this scene, everyone in the sleepy little college town of Harper knows who Welles really is. Loretta Young, his wife, tries to shoot him. She succeeds, but also shoots the clock mechanism, which sets the knight with a sword and the angel it is chasing to travel around the belfry at lethal speeds. Wounded, Welles staggers to the ledge outside where the angel and knight are speeding around, sidesteps the angel, but gets impaled on the knight's sword. Freeing himself, he pushes the knight off the ledge and then, mortally wounded, falls to his death. A very satisfying ending and one that goes into the clock scene record book as the first time a clock ever stabbed an actor.

The last line of this film has always puzzled clock scene fans and made them wonder if Edward G. Robinson, who was responsible for catching Welles, wasn't a bit of a sadist. After telling Loretta Young her husband is a Nazi and watching her shoot him, see him getting skewered by a clock and then fall 500 feet to his death, he says to her, "Pleasant dreams."

57

Didn't Clifton Webb know that when you play with shotguns around clocks, clocks are bound to get hurt? Scene from *Laura* (1944).

Wild Strawberries (1957). Though Ingmar Bergman's films are not in vogue at the moment, the clock scene in this movie about an elderly professor reviewing his life remains timeless. It takes place in a dream sequence when the protagonist is walking though a town and sees a steeple clock with no hands. One needn't be a clock scene fan to know that a clock without hands symbolizes death. Clock scene fans, however, are not the best people to ask if the clock symbol in this Bergman film was accurate, since they always leave after the clock scene and haven't seen the end of this film yet.

――――――――――――

Laura (1944). Although the sudden demise of Clifton Webb's clock has been clearly established as "death by misadventure," clock scene fans still consider it clock murder and cannot forgive Clifton Webb for blasting it with his shotgun. Didn't Webb know that when you play with shotguns around clocks, clocks are bound to get hurt? Dana Andrews is not very popular in clock scene circles, either. Didn't he know that by shooting Webb while Webb was pointing a shotgun, it was likely to go off? Gene Tierney has a lot to answer for as well. Why wasn't she home when Webb came to murder her?

It is the clock who is the only innocent party in the entire dirty affair. Is there anyone, anywhere, who thinks that it deserved to be blown apart by Webb after allowing Webb to hide the instrument of its death in its inner workings? Oh, it's a great clock scene, all right, but the award was given with a very heavy heart.

CUTLERY

BEST SCENES

Spellbound (1945). Gregory Peck, a favorite actor of many film fans, is no favorite of cutlery scene fans. The reason for their displeasure is the scene in which he is dining with Ingrid Bergman at the sanitorium. As she is talking, Bergman absentmindedly runs a fork over the table linen. Peck keeps staring at the lines the fork makes in the linen. Visibly upset, he suddenly shouts, "There must be a surplus of table linen in this institution."

Now, by the rules of table etiquette, Bergman should never have used a fork that way and Peck was probably correct in reprimanding her. But to a cutlery scene fan, it was Bergman who was correct and Peck the poor sport. Not only did Bergman use her cutlery in a striking and original way, but had she not used it that way, she never would have discovered that, to Peck, the table linen represented snow and the lines the fork made, ski trails. More importantly, Peck would never have remembered what he saw in the snow that day.

Splash (1984). Whenever the importance of cutlery scenes in film is questioned, cutlery scene apologists point to the restaurant scene in which Darryl Hannah orders a lobster. With a complete table setting in front of her, she eats the lobster without cutlery. The fact that she eats the shell is bad enough, but that she eats the shell without using a knife and fork puts it in the disgusting range. When confronted by those who say the scene was inserted by Ron Howard, the film's director, because he wanted to show the world what films would be like without cutlery, cutlery scene fans merely smile and offer no comment.

How Green Was My Valley (1941). Roddy McDowall not only knew his way around a good bird scene, he could handle himself in a dramatic knife and fork scene as well. The cutlery scene between him and his father (Donald Crisp) in the early part of the film is a masterpiece of timing and nuance. When McDowall's older brothers leave the supper table after a dispute with Crisp, he remains to show his Dad he still loves him. How does McDowall express this feeling without words? He bangs his knife and fork on his plate after each mouthful. After three or four bangings, Crisp looks up from his supper and quietly says, "I see you there, my son." Cutlery scene fans, not accustomed to seeing a knife and fork used to express love and devotion, can often be seen weeping with emotion whenever this powerful scene is shown.

DENTIST

BEST SCENES

Marathon Man (1976). Though it does not take place in a dentist's office, the Dustin Hoffman–Laurence Olivier drilling scene in this John Schlesinger film is enormously popular with dentist scene fans. Unfortunately, the inclusion of this harrowing scene on the list does not make dentist scene fans very popular with dentists. Resigned to the fact that they are often portrayed as villains, many dentists are particularly unhappy that Olivier uses the novocaine after the drilling, not before, as they are taught to do in dental school. They are also upset by the fact that since the release of this film no dentist has been able to ask a patient, "Is it safe?"

Little Shop of Horrors (1986). To a dentist scene fan it has everything – a patient so frightened he can hang from the ceiling, another, who when asked to say "ah," cries "argh!" after he sees what is in store for him, and Steve Martin playing a sadistic dentist with all the stops pulled out. Martin finally meets his match when a masochistic patient, played, with all the stops jerked out, by Bill Murray, walks into his office. Murray can't wait to be drilled. In this inspired scene he even adjusts the dentist's light and puts in the cotton rolls himself so Martin can get started inflicting pain sooner. Best moment: a tossup between Murray trying to steal a drill on his way out and Martin punching his nurse

63

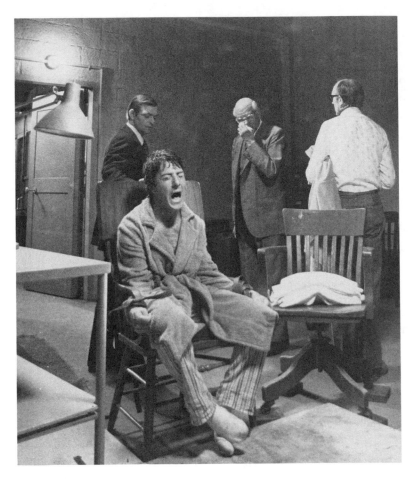

Dustin Hoffman wasn't particularly happy that Laurence Olivier used the novocaine after the drilling, not before, as he was taught to do in dental school, in the film _Marathon Man_ (1976).

while singing, "Be a dentist! You have a talent for causing pain." Best line: "Wait, I'm not numb."

_10_ (1979). Dentist scene fans are still disappointed with

Blake Edwards for changing the title of his movie about a man's yen for a dentist's daughter from 5 to 10. It was originally called 5 because that was how many fillings Dudley Moore had to submit to in order to get Bo Derek's honeymoon address. The result was tough on Moore but a treat for dentist scene fans who get to watch a rarity in movies – a five-filling dentist scene.

What finally softened up dentist scene fans enough to vote the scene into the awards category was its residual effects. After leaving the dentist's office, Moore can't drink coffee because he has a mouth full of novocaine; he's unable to talk to Julie Andrews because he has a mouth full of novocaine; and he nearly gets arrested when he can't tell the police he has a mouth full of novocaine because he has a mouth full of novocaine. One sure way to spot a dentist scene fan, by the way, is if you ever hear someone refer to this film as 5.

ELEVATOR

B E S T   S C E N E S

Trading Places (1983). Elevator scene fans were surprised and delighted to get a glimpse of a vase of flowers inside the elevator that Eddie Murphy steps out from on his first day in his new job as a commodities trader. Until that moment, a chair and a mirror were the best elevator scene fans could expect in terms of elevator interior design. Elevator scene historians report that with this sly elevator comedy, filmmakers became aware of elevator interiors as a mark of power and wealth. What can we expect in elevator design in future films? Elevator scene interior decorators predict that the next step in elevator ostentation will probably be a working fireplace. When these begin to appear it is fairly certain that the elevator string quartet will not be too far behind.

The Man with Two Brains (1983). The two greatest fears of elevator passengers – getting stuck between floors and being stuck with a hypodermic needle filled with cleaning fluid – are dealt with in this absorbing elevator movie. The result is a series of elevator scenes that keep elevator scene fans in a perpetual state of levitation. The elevator action takes place in Vienna, where Steve Martin takes his bride, Kathleen Turner, on a belated honeymoon. First the hotel elevator repeatedly stops be-tween floors, so elevator scene fans are treated to the sight of

Martin climbing down from elevators that stopped too soon, and up from elevators that stopped too late.

Adding to the excitement is a deranged elevator killer who periodically injects luckless passengers with cleaning fluid. Why cleaning fluid? So the brain of the injected passenger is the last thing to die. (This is one of the questions invariably asked on the elevator fan club entrance exam.) In addition to its award, elevator fans have voted this movie one of the two most exciting elevator movies in film history.

**Class (1983). Though this scene never got by the Uplift Committee (an ad hock group trying to protect the morals of elevator scene fans), it had enough support to win honorable mention. The scene in question is the one in which Jacqueline Bisset and Andrew McCarthy (her son's best friend) make love in a glass elevator that runs outside a building. A highly-placed source in the elevator scene fan club reports that the Uplift Committee is slated to be disbanded at the next elevator scene fan club meeting. According to this unnamed source, a majority of the members feel that any group which allows elevator murder and bans elevator lovemaking may not be doing such a good job.

The Turning Point (1978). This film, which is reported to have done so much for the popularity of ballet in America, didn't do too badly for the popularity of elevators, either. The scene that did it for elevators occurs midway through the film. Leslie Browne has just downed six Manhattans because she discovered Mikhail Baryshnikov with another dancer. On her way back to give a performance, there is a quick cut to Anne Bancroft waiting for the backstage elevator. The elevator doors open on Leslie Browne sitting on the floor quite drunk. She even waves, "Hi."

Elevator scene historians believe this is the first time someone not dead was shown sitting in an elevator. Particularly satisfying to elevator etiquette buffs is the fact that Browne was sitting facing the door. To those who ask what did this film actually do for the popularity of elevators, elevator scene statisticians point to this datum: In the year this movie was released, elevator travel was up 120 percent.

Dressed to Kill (1980). Angie Dickinson has done for elevators what Janet Leigh did for showers – she made people afraid to go into one. It is no secret that there was a lot of support for consigning this scene for film oblivion – the reason being that elevator scene fans do not ordinarily favor elevator scenes which show elevators in a bad light. Still, elevator murder is most rare, and when tastefully done it can be quite thrilling. This is why they agreed to consider it. The vote was close, the deciding factor being director Brian De Palma's stylish handling of the stabbing, which was accomplished without messing up the interior of the elevator. It is interesting to note that in *Psycho* (1960), Hitchcock doesn't let his victim mess up the shower, either. Elevator scene moralists like to point to two other similarities between these two films – both murderers are dressed as women and both actresses play characters who are carrying on an illicit affair.

The Pink Panther (1964). Even rarer than elevator murder is elevator dressing. (This is elevator scene fan parlance for an elevator that is used as a wardrobe.) It is pulled off quite smartly by Inspector Clouseau's wife, the beautiful actress Capucine. After being spotted by the Paris police, she quickly ducks into an office building elevator, turns her suit jacket inside out, changes her hat, shoes and handbag, and emerges from the same elevator in a completely different outfit. Elevator scene fans have attempted to duplicate Capucine's performance in a variety of elevators throughout the nation, but to date have been unable to report any great success.

Big Business (1988). Having just recovered from Angie Dickinson's stabbing in *Dressed to Kill* (1980), elevator scene fans are confronted with a near dog-garroting in this occasionally funny movie about elevator pet safety. The unfortunate incident (meant to be a lesson to dog owners) occurs after Lily Tomlin befriends a stray dog so she can take it for its first elevator ride. Tomlin, demonstrating a prime elevator-dog "DON'T DO THIS" rule, has tied a makeshift silk leash around the dog's neck. When the elevator doors open she gets out but the dog doesn't, breaking another "DON'T DO THIS" rule. Horrified, Tomlin watches the doors close and the leash disappears into the crack in the elevator door.

Luckily this was only a pet safety demonstration and before even the most faint-hearted elevator scene fan can faint, the doors open back up and the dog walks out angry but unharmed. It immediately becomes obvious that the dog was no stray, but an accomplished pet-safety performer, trained to push the "stop" button should something go wrong.

Lady in a Cage (1964). Elevators have feelings, too. That is the premise of this disturbing thriller starring Olivia De Havilland and James Caan (his screen debut). When the elevator in De Havilland's mansion breaks down with her inside, she reprimands it very sharply by exclaiming, "Oh, what's the matter with you?" This resulted in an elevator huff, which resulted in De Havilland being trapped in a sulking elevator. She didn't like this at all because all sorts of people break into the house and terrorize her. Elevator scene fans like it though, because the elevator is on screen practically the entire movie. Best moment: When De Havilland throws her shoe through the elevator bars at the ringing telephone (a movie first).

There are a number of other actors who knew the ups and

downs of a good elevator scene. Among them are Keenan Wynn and Shirley MacLaine, who played the role of elevator operators: Wynn, as Gregory Peck's former sergeant in *The Man in the Gray Flannel Suit* (1956), and MacLaine, as Fred MacMurray's mistress in *The Apartment* (1960). An actor who hated elevators but is loved by elevator scene fans is Zero Mostel. Mostel is crammed into one of the smallest elevators in screen history with Gene Wilder and a very effeminate assistant director in *The Producer* (1968) and then nearly pushed down an elevator shaft in *The Hot Rock* (1972).

An actress held in especially high regard by elevator scene fans for her uncanny ability to publicize elevators is Audrey Hepburn. While playing the role of Princess Ann in *Roman Holiday* (1953), she walks into Gregory Peck's room after escaping from her castle, takes one look at it, and casually remarks, "Is this the elevator?" Elevator statisticians report that the year following that remark there was an estimated 43 percent increase in Hollywood elevator scenes.

FALSE TEETH

B E S T   S C E N E S

Crossing Delancey (1987). Though Hollywood's lack of courage in this genre had limited false teeth scenes mostly to shots of them in half-filled glasses of water, it hasn't stopped actors with the right false teeth sensibility from occasionally turning one into a scene that thrills the audience. That is precisely what happens when Amy Irving's bubba gives Peter Reichart his whiskey in a glass containing a set of lowers. Reichart, who could have ruined the scene by going "Yecch," instead made it immortal with the reaction of an actor who truly knows his way around a false teeth scene. When she hands him the glass, he calmly remarks, "I said whiskey neat, not on the rocks."

Midnight Cowboy (1969). On the rare occasion when a false teeth scene escaped from its glass of water, it took an ugly encounter between the normally sweet Jon Voight and the normally sweet Bernard Hughes to pull it off. While the shot of Hughes's false teeth coming loose after Voight hit him for nonpayment of services rendered is considered a false teeth classic, false teeth fans would have settled for Hughes biting into an apple to get the shot. This admission took a certain amount of courage. It was an admission that false teeth fans, lulled by too many shots of uppers and lowers in too many glasses of water, were not yet ready for a false teeth scene in the midst of a homosexual encounter.

Starting Over (1979). While false teeth fans prefer to see an actual denture, they are not averse to scenes in which false teeth are merely mentioned, as long as they are mentioned in a favorable light. A good example of this occurs in the final scene of this very appealing comedy when Burt Reynolds asks Jill Clayburgh to marry him. In his proposal, he lists all the things he would like to do together with Clayburgh, including a wish to see their dentures in the same glass when they are old. "That's what I want. What do you want?" Reynolds asks. Clayburgh then responds with a line that endeared her to health conscious false teeth fans everywhere. "I want my own glass," she says.

For the record, marriage proposal scenes did put in a claim for this scene, but it was quickly dropped when false teeth scene fans, normally possessive about their territory, threatened to have every actor and actress in every winning marriage proposal scene checked for dentures.

A Clockwork Orange (1971). Stanley Kubrick, normally quite an interesting director, let false teeth scene fans down somewhat when he decided to stick with a classic but unadventurous false-teeth-in-the-glass-of-water-scene in this otherwise original film. When a school official visits Malcolm McDowall to let him know what kind of trouble he's in, the official is so upset that he needs a glass of water. He reaches over to the bedtable and when he drinks, sees McDowall's mother's teeth in the glass. There are only two possible reasons for the appearance of this scene on the list: Kubrick's reputation, and the desperate shortage of really first-rate false teeth scenes in Hollywood.

Help! (1965). When the crazed-looking man in the Beatles's apartment releases two sets of fake false teeth that go chattering across the rug toward the camera, some film fans felt it was just a cheap attempt to get a laugh. False teeth fans find this attitude ridiculous and insulting – another example of how people put down the genre. To them, it seemed obvious that both the man and the false teeth had a role to play. The man is a dowser and the false teeth were looking for a glass of water.

FLUTTERING DRAPE

B E S T　　S C E N E S

Lost Horizons (1937). In Hollywood, fluttering drapes have been used to symbolize many things, the most interesting being the death of Sam Jaffe. In this distinguished film set in Shangri-La, fluttering drape fans are quick to point out that when Jaffe (as the high lama) finally gives up the ghost, it is the flutterring drapes, not the candle going out, that tips off Ronald Colman and the audience that Jaffe is dead. Admirers of this memorable scene credit the movie's director, Frank Capra, with such great camera work that one can almost see Jaffe's soul floating out the window.

The Uninvited (1947). By the time this film was made, fluttering drape scenes had so evolved that they were able to bring to a stop both haunting crying sounds and the smell of mimosa. Every night, when Gail Russell went to sleep, she heard the crying and smelled the mimosa. The crying and the smell of mimosa went on all night until the dawn breeze made the drapes on her windows flutter. When the drapes began to flutter the crying and the smell of mimosa stopped. Russell was very grateful. It meant she could finally get to sleep.

The World of Henry Orient (1964). A set designer's goof

nearly cost this charming movie its rightful place in the fluttering drape history. The scene nearly lost to us is the Peter Sellers–Paula Prentiss "fluttering drape seduction scene." It appears in quotes because the drapes never fluttered. The drapes never fluttered because a distracted set designer (his car having been towed away that morning) misread the word "diaphanous" as "denim." As a result, Sellers had to peak through the drapes to spot Tippy Walker and Merrie Spaeth sitting on the steps across the street. The original shooting script has Sellers spotting them through fluttering, diaphanous drapes. Only the chance discovery of the now retired set designer's diary saved this scene from oblivion.

Rebecca (1940). Had it not been for the fluttering drapes in this Academy Award winner, Joan Fontaine might have listened to Mrs. Danvers and jumped from her bedroom window. Judith Anderson, who played Mrs. Danvers, had some pretty strong arguments. Laurence Olivier would never have loved her as he did the first Mrs. DeWinter. And, it would have been so easy to jump. Fontaine was about to jump, but the fluttering of the window drapes distracted and brought her to her senses. That is the opinion of a surprising number of fluttering drape fans, many of whom have seen this scene over a dozen times. A small number of fans are of the opinion that Alfred Hitchcock, the film's director, may have wanted Fontaine to jump and reshot the scene without drapes. Reports of fans' seeing this drapeless version still circulate in fluttering drape circles.

The Turning Point (1978). Though fluttering drapes may never replace crashing waves as the place a camera with a sense of delicacy can turn to when two people are making love, they have been used on occasion. They are used to great advantage when the camera cuts to them while Mikhail Baryshnikov makes

In Hollywood, fluttering drapes have been used to symbolize many things, the most interesting being the death of Sam Jaffe in _Lost Horizons_ (1937).

love to Leslie Browne for the first time. Fluttering drape followers are especially fond of this film because one can sit through this entire movie and not see one venetian blind.

Black Narcissus (1946). When Deborah Kerr tells David Farrar, "It's the wind," her words are enough to set the heart

Fluttering drape fans loved _Turning Point_ (1977). There wasn't a venetian blind in the entire movie.

of even the most casual fluttering drape scene fan aflutter. Kerr is trying to explain the cause of the sexual tension she and the sisters are experiencing in that convent so high in the Himalayas. But fluttering drape scene fans aren't interested in that sort of stuff. They are interested in wind, one of the two main elements of a good fluttering drape scene.

Since the wind in this part of the Himalayas blows seven days a week, all that remains to get a good fluttering drape scene is drapes. Happily, there are more drapes in this mountaintop convent than a fluttering drape fan can shake a curtain rod at. We learn as much during the opening scene when Ayah, the old caretaker, is seen running through the remote mountain mission while the camera catches every fluttering drape on every window.

**The wind in this part of the Himalayas blew seven days a week in
Black Narcissus (1946).**

From that point on there is hardly a scene in which a drape does
not flutter. They are used quite nicely to heighten the already
charged atmosphere and play a key role in the scene in which one
of the sisters goes mad.

Most fluttering drape scene fans consider this to be one of the
most satisfying fluttering drape films in recent memory. I
wholeheartedly agree, and would like to add a footnote. During
a late night viewing of this remarkable film, I discovered
something I had completely forgotten. Since this and my last
viewing, I had gotten it into my head that the title of the movie
came from one of the flowers that Flora Robeson grew in her
garden. I was wrong. It is named after a cheap scent that Sabu
had bought in an army-navy store in London.

FOOD MUSHING
B E S T S C E N E S

The Treasure of the Sierra Madre (1948). Nobody knew how to push beans around a plate like Walter Huston, who in his heyday was the only bankable food-mushing superstar in Hollywood. Food mushing fans say that Huston was so good that if you listened carefully, you could hear a definite contrapuntal rhythm between his fork scraping the metal plate and his repeated food-mushing entreaties to Tim Holt and Humphrey Bogart as they sit around the campfire. "Want some beans?" Scrape, scrape. "Better have some beans, boys." Scrape, scrape, scrape. "You sure you won't have some beans?" Scrape, scrape. It is a memorable food-mushing moment and one that makes it clear that if Holt and Bogart had been eating their beans, they wouldn't have been too exhausted to sit around the campfire and mush food with Huston.

Sitting Pretty (1948). The food mushing scene in this film is so seductive that even the urbane Clifton Webb finds it impossible not to join the fun. Though Webb never cracks a smile, food mushing fans insist he enjoyed it even when the baby throws cereal at him. Webb's lips do form what appears to be a smirk when he retaliates and dumps a bowl of cereal on the baby's head. Food mushing fans explain Webb's rare show of emotion this way: Watching food being mushed is never as much fun as mushing it yourself.

Nobody knew how to push beans around a plate like Walter Huston in *The Treasure of the Sierra Madre* (1948).

Of Mice and Men (1939). Food mushing scenes can also be dangerous. Bob Steele finds that out in this classic study of what watching milk being mixed with apple pie can do to someone who is dull-witted. The award winning scene is wonderfully orchestrated by director Lewis Milestone.

First, Steele pours the milk over his apple pie with a great show. Then, he starts to mush it up with his spoon. From Steele's expression it's easy to see he knows this will infuriate Lennie (played by Lon Chaney, Jr.) but he hasn't the remotest idea how much. This is only the midpoint of the action and already food mushing fans are anticipating the next dish. They do not have long to wait. A few seconds later, Lennie crushed the hand Steele used to mush his milk and apple pie to a pulp. Considered an

84

especially nice touch is Milestone's use of the apple pie and milk combination to foreshadow the coming violence.

Charlie Bubbles (1968). Food mushing scenes that take place in trendy London restaurants are a special favorite of food mushing fans. The food mushing scene in this movie is caused by writer jealousy and pits two old friends – Albert Finney, a successful writer, and Colin Blakely, an unsuccessful writer – against one another. The food mushing starts over dessert when Finney pushes whipped cream in Blakely's face. Blakely retaliates with crème brûlèe in Finney's face. The food mushing continues through the dessert menu until both writers wind up walking out of the restaurant covered with food.

Food mushing fans all agree that with the release of this film a peak has been reached in this genre and a standard set that all food mushing scenes should be judged against. They also agree that they particularly like it when all the sentences in a review of a food mushing scene begin with or contain the words, "food mushing."

Papillon (1973). Some food mushing scenes are not for the fainthearted. This is especially true when they are set in a solitary confinement cell on Devil's Island. Food mushing fans, however, are not easily revolted. So when Steve McQueen is put on half rations for not squealing on Dustin Hoffman, he shows he can mush food in a revolting way with the best of them. The fact that the "food" he mushes is beetles and grasshoppers in no way violates rule 3 in the newly revised Food Mushing Manual. In essence, rule 3 states that to be eligible for a food mushing award, an actor may mush anything as long as it is eventually eaten.

Brighton Beach Memoirs (1986). Where else would you

expect to find the most original food mushing moment in film history but in Brooklyn? More specifically, the Brooklyn of Neil Simon's boyhood, circa 1937. But even in Brooklyn, great food mushing scenes aren't that easy to put together. First, liver has to be on the menu for dinner. Then, the liver has to be tough and it has to be served with mashed potatoes. Then, the actor it's served to (Jonathan Silverman) has to not like liver and bury it in his mashed potatoes when he thinks his mother isn't looking. Finally, he has to have a sharp-eyed mother (Blythe Danner), who tells him to eat the liver under his mashed potatoes. Funniest exchange? When Danner says to her son, "Why did you take the liver if you didn't like it?" and her son replies, "I didn't take it. It came with the plate."

The Magnificent Ambersons (1942). To a food mushing scene fan, the character of the food musher has never been a consideration. What counts is the quality of the food mushing. So, even though Tim Holt is a spoiled, self-centered son who ruins his mother's chance for happiness, his skill at wolfing down his maiden aunt's (Agnes Moorehead) strawberry shortcake is what put this scene over the top. The cake (first of the season) was in such danger of being eaten before the scene was over that Moorehead was prompted to tell Holt not to eat so fast.

No collection of great food mushing scenes would be complete without a special nod to Jeannie Berlin, who in the movie *The Heartbreak Kid* (1972), ordered an egg salad sandwich on her honeymoon and ate it so sloppily that Charles Grodin, her husband of two days, left her to pursue Cybill Shepherd. Though sloppily eaten sandwiches are not technically food mushing scenes, it was felt that Berlin's sacrifice to the art of food mushing should be noted.

This cleared the way for a special food mushing award to be

Public Enemy **(1931) sets the standard by which all food mushing scenes are judged.**

given Gene Hackman, who in *The French Connection* (1970), had the grace not to be overly annoyed at having to gobble down a street vendor's hot dog while watching drug smuggler Fernando Rey through a restaurant window dining on what looks to be a pretty decent French meal.

This made the ritual toast to James Cagney (smashing a half-grapefruit into the face of the person on your left) all the more poignant. Cagney, of course, is the actor who "smushed" the first half-grapefruit into Mae Clark's face when she began to nudge him in *Public Enemy* (1931). The scene is now considered to be the standard by which all other food mushing scenes are judged.

FUNNY WALK

B E S T S C E N E S

To Have and Have Not (1944). Fans of funny walks like to say that Walter Brennan practiced his funny walk so much that he knew it backwards and forwards. That is literally true. In one marvelous scene Brennan does his funny walk forwards and backwards in the same scene and makes it seem fresh both times. He does it forwards on his way into the bar to ask Humphrey Bogart for drink money and backwards away from the bar when he sees Bogart being escorted out by the Vichy police. Funny walk fans especially appreciate the fact that Brennan was able to reverse his funny walk without missing a beat. They cannot agree, however, whether the walk consisted of two steps and a hop or three steps and a hop. What they did agree on was that it was a very funny walk and the scene is one that is likely to be remembered for a very long time.

Bells of St. Trinian's (1946). Had I not seen a sign on the clubhouse door which read, FUNNY WALK SCENE DEADLINE IS 5 P.M., the funny walk in this British import might have been lost to movie fans forever. As a lapsed member of the funny walk scene fan club, I still had voting privileges, and though I had not seen this film in quite a while, proposed it for an award. I described to my fellow funny walk scene fans a character in this film named "Harry" who I seem to remember was played by Colin Blakely.

89

Harry would wait in the woods outside St. Trinian's for a signal from its headmistress, delightfully played by Alastair Sims. When Sims gave the signal, Harry would put his hands into the pockets of his long overcoat and glide across the lawn to the school. His steps were always in sync with a catchy background tune which was only played when Harry did his walk. When asked to imitate the walk, I could not. Instead, I compared it to a dance performed by the Moiseyev Dance Company in which men in floor-length coats glide across the stage. What made the dance so remarkable was that you never see their legs moving. So it was with Harry's walk. You never see his legs moving.

House Calls (1978). Fans of funny walk scenes have been expecting Walter Matthau to win a funny walk award for more than two decades. No actor ever had such a naturally funny walk or showed so much promise. Unhappily, Matthau never lived up to that promise until he got the opportunity to go jogging with Glenda Jackson. His walk in that scene was so comic and original it earned him this long-awaited laurel and rewarded the patience of funny walk scene fans across the nation. What may have finally put him over the top, report funny walk scene theorists, was Matthau's attempt run in order to keep up with Jackson. I am inclined to agree.

Monty Python and the Holy Grail (1974). The sound of horses' hooves in the mist is not a very promising situation in which to find a funny walk. Nor is the sight of knights' heads bobbing as they come over the rise. But if, when they finally appear in full view, it turns out to be John Cleese leading a group of knights who have no horses, the situation is indeed promising. Cleese and the knights are not knights on horseback at all, they are imitating knights on horseback by walking funny.

At this point it might be worth noting that the selection of

90

this scene caused quite a heated discussion. Many funny walk scene fans have not yet forgiven Cleese for his "Ministry of Silly Walks" skit on public television. Since "Silly Walks" was aired, funny walk scene club members have become the butt of many jokes. That club members were able to rise above their personal feelings and select this scene show that funny walk scene fans take funny walks seriously. What may finally have clinched it for Cleese were the men following behind the knights banging coconuts together so the funny walks would sound like horses galloping.

The Hunchback of Notre Dame (1939). Quasimodo's goofy walk as he follows Esmeralda through the streets of 15th century Paris greatly endeared Charles Laughton to funny walk scene fans here in the United States. Funny walk scene insiders report there are two theories to explain the origin of Laughton's funny walk. The first, and most widely held, is that it was caused by Laughton's fake hump, which may have thrown off his gait. The second theory, just recently formulated, is that Laughton sprained his ankle while lying on his back ecstatically kicking the bells after Maureen O'Hara gave him a drink of water on the pillory. This theory was formed when it was noticed that Laughton began favoring his left leg, transforming his walk into a definite lope. Since Laughton kept no funny walk diary, it is unlikely that either theory will ever be proved.

Young Frankenstein (1974). That funny walk scene fans should choose a funny walk scene based on one of the oldest jokes in history shows they have no shame. Still, when it is done right, the old "Walk this way," routine can result in a very funny walk. When Marty Feldman, who plays Igor carrying a very short cane, tells Gene Wilder to "walk this way," and then bends over each time he uses the cane, funny walk scene fans howl. When Wilder

91

just follows him, prompting Feldman to say, "No, walk *this* way," and demonstrates, they howl even louder. When Wilder finally walks the way Feldman walks, they are convulsed. Funny walk scene historians report that the question, "What would people think of this selection?" never came up during the voting. Apparently, there is just one thing that counts in a funny walk scene – *is the walk funny?* It is.

(It should be mentioned here that the character "Igor" is based on the character "Fritz," young Frankenstein's servant in the original 1931 version of this film, *Frankenstein*. Fritz also had a short cane and used it much like Feldman did. At some point in the film, the cane mysteriously disappears and so does Fritz's funny walk. Funny walk scene fans are now reasonably certain they were found by Mel Brooks.)

Mr. Hulot's Holiday (1954). A favorite of funny walk scene fans since he began walking funny in *Jour de Fête* (1949), Jacques Tati's funny walk reached its peak in this joyous French comedy. Tati's self-conscious walk (on tip toes, with his upper body forward) is best described by imagining what a rather shy ostrich would look like if he were unsure of where he was going or whether he would be welcome when he arrived. Tati is so revered by funny walk scene fans, they saved his funny walk scene for last.

Though film shorts are not permitted on the ballot, the funny walk scene steering committee has given me special permission to mention a funny walk scene I saw some years ago in a film called *The Existentialist*. It had no dialogue, just one man walking in the street rather deliberately. He is walking forwards, and everyone else in the film is walking backwards. In one particularly amusing scene a woman tries to get him to walk backwards like everyone else, but fails. Funny walk scene stunt experts have explained to me that the funny walk effect was achieved by having the man walk backwards and then running the film backwards, a trick that would make it appear he was walking forward and everyone else was walking backwards. I have never believed them, preferring to believe everyone in the film was indeed walking backwards except the hero.

HAIRCUT

B E S T   S C E N E S

The Treasure of the Sierra Madre (1948). Who would have thought that Humphrey Bogart would have such exquisite barbershop manners? The haircut he receives in that Mexican barbershop may just be one of the three worst haircuts in Western film history. Yet, when the barber shows Bogart how it looks in the back, he meekly nods, okay. Why?

Some haircut scene fans simply feel that Bogart didn't want to hurt the barber's feelings. Others feel that director, John Huston, held Bogart in a tight rein in order to make his anger against Tim Holt more convincing. But a growing minority of haircut scene fans explain Bogart's blind acceptance of "the haircut," as it is now referred to in haircut scene circles, by theorizing Bogart didn't care how he looked because he knew he wasn't going to make it out of the film alive.

Yellowbeard (1986). Haircut scene fans are no dummies. Once they discover that Yellowbeard's son has committed a treasure map to memory and tattooed it to the top of his head in case he forgets where the treasure map is, they knew this otherwise unremarkable pirate spoof would contain a remarkable haircut scene. They were right, it did, and it comes with surprising swiftness. When Yellowbeard's son shows a lapse of memory at the wrong moment, Yellowbeard (Graham Chapman) takes out his saber and gives his son what may be the fastest and funniest haircut in screen history.

―――――――

Hannah and Her Sisters (1985). Maureen O'Sullivan is beloved by haircut scene fans for delivering what they consider to be the best haircut line in haircut film history. Turning to her husband Lloyd Nolan, she refers to him as "This haircut that passes for a man." In one devastating line, O'Sullivan was able to evoke all the expensive haircuts Nolan took during their troubled marriage in order to look better to all the women he had affairs with. Since there is no mention in the Haircut Scene Rule Book about a haircut scene actually having to be in a movie to be eligible, the scene was voted into film on the strength of a single line of dialogue.

―――――――

Jailhouse Rock (1957). One of the best examples of haircut foreshadowing occurs in this early Elvis Presley movie when a woman at a bar says to Presley, "You got nice hair." Before we know it, Presley is in his cell waiting to get a haircut.

The tension heightens markedly when his cellmate, Mickey Shaughnessy, tells Presley that prison barbers being what they are, it will cost him three packs of cigarettes to get a good haircut.

It is at this point in the film that haircut scene fans in the audience usually throw cigarette packs at the screen. Some of these must have gotten to the barber who gives good haircuts. Because when Presley gets his haircut (a scene which lasts all of three seconds) he just gets a little taken off the sides. Not to worry. Whatever was taken off grows back remarkably quickly (in the next ten minutes). All of which tends to leave haircut scene fans unsatisfied, but puts Presley fans into a state of near bliss, since his singing seems to improve at the same rate his hair grows back.

Roman Holiday (1953). Tullio Carminati, Audrey Hepburn's Italian barber, was so impressed with the haircut he gave her that he asked Hepburn to go dancing. This barber-customer date is a screen first, not repeated again until *Shampoo* in 1975. Haircut scene fans were especially impressed with Carminati's ability to sweat while cutting Hepburn's hair (to show he didn't approve of how much she wanted to take off). Carminati's use of the word "off" each time he takes a snip and his repeatedly asking Hepburn, "Are you sure, Miss?" nearly won him a Golden Scissors award. Haircut scene purists who require a good haircut before voting a scene its award needn't have worried. Not even the Demon Barber of Fleet Street could make Audrey Hepburn look anything less than lovely.

Wizard of Oz (1939). Haircut scene fans are continuously amazed how in a film which features witches, wizards and flying monkeys there is room for a nifty little haircut scene. It occurs when Dorothy (Judy Garland), the Cowardly Lion (Bert Lahr), the Tin Man (Jack Haley), Scarecrow (Ray Bolger) and Toto reach the Emerald City. Bolger gets more straw, Lahr gets his mane permed and ribbons added, Haley gets a Simonize, and Garland gets her hair cut and curled. Even Toto gets spruced up.

Each "haircut" is performed to the accompaniment of a delightful song. In one song the lyrics include the classic haircut line, "With a snip, snip here, and a snip, snip there." Another song blends the familiar haircut words, "Snip, snip, snip," with "Buzz, buzz, buzz." Though the lady barbers sing a good haircut, not a lock of hair seems to be cut. Still, when confronted with a haircut scene of such charm, and one that included what is generally regarded as the first dog haircut in screen history, not even the staunchest of haircut scene purists objected to its award.

In a special ceremony that took place after the voting, a pair

97

of Golden Scissors awards were given out for uncommon valor during a haircut. The first went to Gregory Peck for his superb work in *The Omen* (1976). While giving his son a haircut, Peck continued to cut after discovering the "666" he suspected was on the boy's scalp was actually there, marking his son as the Antichrist. A second Golden Scissors went to a very young Dean Stockwell, who in *The Boy with Green Hair* (1948), agreed to have his head shaven when nobody liked the color green his hair turned. A few silent tears were noted by the awards panel, but given Stockwell's age at the time, it did not affect their admiration.

Before finally adjourning, haircut scene fans also awarded Dirk Bogarde a rare Bronze Scissor. Bogarde (*A Death in Venice*, 1971) won this honor for his courage in remaining in Venice to keep a barbershop appointment even though he knew there was an outbreak of typhus in the city. The award was given posthumously, since Bogarde lost his life on the Lido beach in a beautifully acted final moment, with much of the barber's recently applied mascara running down his face.

INVITATION REFUSAL

B E S T   S C E N E S

The Razor's Edge (1957). The actor invitation refusal scene fans regard as the doyen of invitation refusers is Clifton Webb. In this pre–Bill Murray version of the Somerset Maugham novel, Webb puts so much effort into his refusal of an invitation to the Riviera "A-list" party of the year that it literally kills him. Admirers of the scene still remember the tactfully worded letter of regret dictated to Tyrone Power in which Webb said he "was unable to attend because of a previous appointment with his maker." They were his last words.

The irony that Webb had not actually been invited to the party and that Power had to steal the invitation was not lost on invitation refusal scene experts. But it did not dampen their admiration of Webb's ultimate sacrifice to the genre.

The Egyptian (1954). The only known case of a film actor who offered an invitation *and* refused its acceptance is pulled off by Bella Darvi. Darvi, a popular ancient Egyptian courtesan, promises Edmond Purdom, a young ancient Egyptian medical student, that she will show him perfection in love. When Purdom accepts the invitation, first hocking his parents' prepayment to the embalmers of the House of the Dead in order to raise money for her fee, Darvi refuses to accept Purdom's acceptance of her invitation. To be fair, Darvi claims that by refusing to go to bed with Purdom, she *was* showing him perfection in love. Invitation refusal fans didn't buy that at all and voted the scene into the refusal category unanimously. As for Purdom, he spent the next seven years working in the House of the Dead to pay for his parents' funeral.

_____

The Quiet Man (1952). Invitation refusal fans get special pleasure when a scene they know was headed for the marriage proposal genre gets sidetracked into their bailiwick. This is one reason they regard Victor McLaglen so highly. McLaglen's ability not to be buffaloed by John Wayne in a bowler hat or swayed by Barry Fitzgerald's charming introduction of "Sean Thornton, bachelor, to Mary Kate Dennehy, spinster" counted for a lot when the final votes were cast.

So powerful was McLaglen's refusal of Wayne's invitation to Maureen O'Hara that it caused Wayne to spend the next few months riding his black stallion over the Irish countryside like a wild man. A small group of invitation refusal enthusiasts, who still study the words McLaglen used in his eventual acceptance of Wayne's invitation ("I'm permitting this man to court me sister"), contend they reveal that McLaglen was still against the match.

LAUGHING

BEST SCENES

The Pink Panther Strikes Again (1976). The question is still being discussed in laughing scene fan circles: Is Herbert Lom laughing because he is trying to kill Peter Sellers? Is he laughing because the room is filled with laughing gas? Or is he laughing because Peter Sellers's fake nose is melting off? Being a very easygoing group, laughing scene fans are not inordinately concerned that they have not found the answer to these questions. Since the scene is definitely a laughing scene, and a very funny one indeed, it was voted in on its merits alone.

Sleeper (1973). A sentimental choice among laughing scene fans is the scene in which Diane Keaton passes the laughing orb around, causing her house robot (Woody Allen) to laugh. Allen's laugh was actually more of a closed-mouthed snicker, as a laugh would have blown his cover.

More than a few laughing scene fans who cast their ballot for this rare screen moment have confessed that they chose the scene because it is the only movie that they can remember Woody Allen laughing in. Armchair laughing scene psychiatrists find it interesting that Allen chose to be a robot when he does finally laugh on screen, something he has no doubt discussed with his analyst.

Quest for Fire (1982). Technical advisors in the caveman laughter subgenre have been advising Hollywood moviemakers to delete laughing scenes from caveman movies for decades. As a result, Victor Mature didn't laugh in *One Million B.C.*, Raquel Welch didn't laugh in the remake of *One Million B.C.*, and Trog didn't laugh in *Trog*. Because Jean-Jacques Annaud, the director of this French import, used no technical advisor, Rae Dawn Chong became the first caveperson in movie history to laugh on film. She laughs when one of the cavemen she is traveling with gets hit in the head by a rock. Her laughter is so catchy, pretty soon all the cavemen with her are laughing, even the one who got hit in the head. The resulting laughing scene is not only very satisfying to laughing scene fans, it received three-and-a-half stars from Roger Ebert.

―――――――――

Sometimes a Great Notion (1971). Richard Jaeckel may be the only actor in movie history to drown laughing. Paul Newman, who starred in and directed this film about the dangers of laughing while underwater, made Jaeckel laugh while trying to feed him air by mouth-to-mouth resuscitation when he was trapped underwater by a fallen log. Jaeckel thought the idea of two grown men kissing underwater was funny. Drowning was the result. Except for a small group of laughing scene fans, few film buffs know about this singular laughing scene. This may be due to the fact the film had two titles, two directors and was not a great box office success. It is hoped that this award will remedy that situation.

―――――――――

The Four Seasons (1981). Laughter at sea (like music) is a wonderful sound to behold. It's not too bad on a lake, either. That is where Alan Alda, Carol Burnett, Jack Weston and Rita Moreno hear their friend Len Cariou making love to his girlfriend, Bess Armstrong, in the cabin on shore. The sounds are loud and graphic. The four friends on the boat do what any civilized persons would do – they try to ignore it. But as the sounds continue, they dissolve into laughter that is so contagious it lifts the scene right into the awards category.

Crimes of the Heart (1986). When Jessica Lange comes back from an all-night date with Sam Shepard she finds Diane Keaton and Sissy Spacek looking pretty glum because they just learned their grandfather is in a coma. So when Lange says she bets that grandpa will go into a coma when he finds out what she's been up to, Spacek and Keaton start to laugh. When they tell her that grandpa already is in a coma, their laughter reaches near hysteria. Which just goes to show you how funny laughter is and how many different things there are to laugh about. Diane Keaton won the special notice of laughing scene fans interested in laughing technique for the snort she perfected in this scene.

Mary Poppins (1964). One of the most unusual laughing scene heroes in the movies is Ed Wynn, who plays Uncle Albert in this magical Disney release. Wynn had the uncanny ability to rise into the air whenever he laughed. Laughing scene auditors report that Wynn did not use a double nor were there any wires holding him up in the scene that won him his award. As for Dick Van Dyke and the two children, the wires were clearly visible. Mary Poppins (Julie Andrews) already knew how to fly.

Wynn was so adept at rising to the ceiling when he laughed, that he often had tea there. It is not generally known, but it is the ambition of every laughing scene club to master Wynn's special skill. Visitors to the laughing scene fan club have often reported hearing the song, "I love to laugh, ha-ha-ha-ha!" coming from the "Laughing Room," where members test their laughing and their levity. To date, no one has discovered Wynn's knack, though many have tried.

103

Kiss of Death (1947). Just when you thought Hollywood would run out of things to laugh at, along comes this low-budget gangster film which catapulted Tommy Udo from a laughing scene cult hero into a star. Udo's high-pitched laughter as he pushes an old lady in a wheelchair down the stairs continues to thrill laughing scene enthusiasts to this day. In an effort to escape from being typecast as a killer who laughs when he does mean things to people, Tommy Udo changed his name to Richard Widmark. Laughing scene fans who have kept track of Udo's career as Richard Widmark have now and then been rewarded with a burst of award-caliber laughter from their hero.

———————

Citizen Kane (1941). A small group of laughing scene fanatics still harbor the notion that if Dorothy Comingore hadn't laughed when Orson Welles got splashed by that puddle, it would have been Welles, not Ronald Reagan who would have been the first President of the United States who had formerly been an actor. Their reasoning is not without merit. If Comingore hadn't laughed when she did: (1) Welles would never have heard her sing; (2) he never would have begun the affair, and (3) he never would have been caught by Big Jim Geddes. This last point cost Welles an election that could have been the stepping stone to the presidency.

Putting historical aspects aside, the scene is also something of a rarity. It may be the only time in film history that an actress laughed while suffering from a toothache. This was the cause of some friction between dentist scene fans and laughing scene fans. It is not generally known, but some years after the film was released, dentist scene fans claimed this scene as their own. At a secret but well-attended meeting between the two groups, it was finally decided that the scene should remain in the "laughing scene" category. There were two overriding reasons: Welles was not a dentist, and Comingore's toothache mysteriously ended without treatment.

104

It's a Mad, Mad, Mad, Mad World (1963). Though the cause of the laughter in this highly-pleasing comedy romp involved one of the oldest jokes in history (someone slipping on a banana peel), no laughing scene fan would ever think of denying it its place in laughing scene history. When Ethel Merman slips on that peel in the hospital where Spencer Tracy, Mickey Rooney, Buddy Hackett, Milton Berle, Terry Thomas, Dick Shawn and Jonathan Winters are lying in casts and splints, no one even thought their laughter mean-spirited. What's more, even though this particular scene is funnier to the actors than to the audience, it was granted its award because from start to finish, the film delivers more belly laughs than any movie ever made.

The actor most beloved by laughing scene fans is Edward Arnold, whose laugh, which sounded something like "gah...geh-geh-geh," is often heard imitated at laughing scene fan get-togethers. (The laughing scene fan able to do the best Edward Arnold laugh imitation is reported to be Ted Williams, the head of a construction firm in New York.) Arnold's distinctive laugh graced such films as *I'm No Angel* (1933), *Cardinal Richelieu* (1935), *Man About Town* (1939), *The Devil and Daniel Webster* (1941), *Meet John Doe* (1941), and *Dear Ruth* (1947). Laughing scene fans report that it's a rare Edward Arnold film in which this laughing scene hero does not get in at least one "gah...geh-geh-geh."

Since the character played by Dudley Moore in *Arthur* (1981) was drunk, the scene was not eligible for an award. Still, many laughing scene fans feel it is certainly worth an honorable mention. Moore's laughter is especially liked by Australian laughing fans who compare it to the call of their native kookaburra bird, which is sometimes affectionately referred to as the "laughing jackass."

MARRIAGE PROPOSAL

BEST SCENES

Little Women (1937). Yes, Paul Lukas actually uses the phrase "dare I hope" in his charming proposal of marriage to Katharine Hepburn in the final scene of this delightfully old-fashioned film. Hepburn knew a great marriage proposal when she saw one. Though Lukas was older, poor and foreign, she accepted immediately. Of course, the rain was a nice touch. So was Lukas's transparent excuse of delivering the book. Apparently, when deciding whether to marry someone, hearing the words "dare I hope" counts for a lot. Marriage proposal scouts have been keeping a watchful eye out for this phrase ever since the release of this classic marriage proposal film. Unhappily, they cannot report ever hearing it used again.

It's a Wonderful Life (1946). Statistics from the Bedford Falls marriage proposal scene fan club reveal that marriages the year this Frank Capra film was released jumped 62 percent. What caused this unusual increase? Many feel it was Donna Reed's refusal to accept Jimmy Stewart's impassioned recital of all the reasons he didn't want to marry her. They theorize that women who saw this scene began to imitate Donna Reed whenever a suitor gave his reason for not wanting to get married. They argue that the large increase in marriages that year was an indication of how deeply this scene affected American women.

107

Marriages jumped the year Jimmy Stewart told Donna Reed all the reasons he didn't want to marry her in *It's A Wonderful Life* (1946).

Even though it worked out okay for Reed and Stewart, some marriage counselors have linked this scene – and the marriages it caused – to the current high rate of divorce.

Three Strangers (1946). Admirers of marriage proposal scenes are an odd lot. They are not inclined to give much weight to the reasons for a proposal of marriage. This may explain the inclusion of Jerome K. Arbutney's proposal to one of his rich and widowed clients in this superb film noir starring Sydney Greenstreet, Peter Lorre and Geraldine Fitzgerald.

At one point in the scene, Arbutney, wonderfully played by

Greenstreet, actually falls to his knees in his zeal to win the lady. Unfortunately,the widow, from whom Greenstreet has been stealing money, had been in touch with her dear departed husband who told her to refuse the offer. This has always been a great disappointment to marriage proposal scene fans since it was the only marriage proposal Greenstreet ever made on screen. Notes from his secret diary confirm what many have long believed. It was this refusal that shattered Greenstreet's confidence and kept him a bachelor in every film he has made since.

North by Northwest (1959). This Hitchcock thriller may be the only film ever made just to get Cary Grant to propose to Eva Marie Saint. Grant is shot at, chased and crop dusted in order to maneuver him into a position where he has to come through with a proposal of marriage. The moment finally arrives when Grant and Saint are hanging from George Washington's head in the Valley of the Presidents being chased by James Mason and his thugs who are out to kill them. Grant carries off the proposal with surprising grace, even though he knew that one false step would send him hurtling to the valley below. Eva Marie Saint's calm acceptance of Grant's proposal isn't bad, either, especially in light of the fact she had told Grant earlier that she got this way because of men like him who didn't want to get married.

Grant, true to his antimarriage feelings to the end, couched his proposal by making it sound like an invitation to ride the train back to New York. Hitchcock has a last laugh, too. Knowing marriage proposal historians would need some sort of marriage confirmation in light of Grant's unclear proposal, he never permits the audience to see the wedding.

Rebecca (1940). One of the truly great marriage proposals in screen history involves a social blunder by the normally correct Sir Laurence Olivier that is compounded by a misunderstanding from the normally sharp-witted Florence Bates. This rare marriage proposal double faux pas occurs when Maxim De Winter, intending to ask Rebecca to be his wife, mistakes Florence Bates for Joan Fontaine, especially in her dealings with Mrs. Danvers (Judith Anderson). Many marriage proposal scene fans feel that Olivier would have been better off marrying Bates, who would have been more of a match for the cruel Mrs. Danvers.

Mildred Pierce (1945). There are a fair number of actresses who have asked men to marry them in movies, but it takes a Joan Crawford to ask a man to ask her to marry him. That's just what Crawford does when she walks in on Zachary Scott after dumping him and proposes to him with the words, "Ask me to marry you." Of course, she was doing it for that arch-spoiled brat of films, her daughter, Veda (Ann Blyth). No dummy, Scott proposes that Crawford give him one-third of the restaurant. Crawford wants Veda back and the price of that is getting Scott back; so she accepts his proposal, in addition to the proposal she proposed in the first place. Had either known what was in store for them, neither would have accepted either of the proposals.

Carnal Knowledge (1971). When Ann-Margret sits on that unmade bed trying to put on her makeup and says to Jack Nicholson, "I want to get married," marriage proposal scene fans in the audience weep openly. "It's a very depressing scene," one marriage proposal scene fan commented after he regained his composure. "Yes, it is," clarified his female companion. "She ends up married to that creep!" It was these differing perceptions of the character Nicholson played that resulted in a curtailment of any discussion of the film after the final vote. Though the male members recognized that Nicholson's attitude toward women wasn't very nice, they couldn't go along when the female members kept referring to him as "the biggest prick in film history."

Crossing Delancey (1988). Before revealing the reason for including this marriage scene in the awards category, three basic marriage proposal rules should be explained: (1) Whether a proposal is accepted is of no importance to the judging panel; (2) The proposal need not be made by the person who wants to get married; (3) It can be made in the presence of others.

Applying these rules to this film we find that – yes, there were other people present besides Peter Riegart and Amy Irving, the woman he loves. Yes, that was Sylvia Miles who actually made the proposal for Riegart. And, yes, Amy Irving refused the proposal. The panel was free to disregard these facts. What they did regard was the fact that Sylvia Miles was eating pickles with her pot roast while she proposed to Irving. Considering Peter Riegart was in the pickle business, this showed great delicacy of feeling to her client (Riegart) and it was this which earned the scene its rightful place in the marriage proposal hall of fame.

———————

The Hunchback of Notre Dame (1939). Probably the most unsentimental proposal of marriage in movie history was made by Maureen O'Hara, as Esmerelda, to Edmond O'Brien, who played Gringoire, in this Hollywood version of the Victor Hugo classic. When O'Hara sees O'Brien about to be hanged by Thomas Mitchell, the King of the Beggar's Union, she asks "Are you going to hang that man?" "Unless you'll take him," Mitchell replies. "I'll take him," says O'Hara. Surprisingly, this three-word proposal of marriage struck a responsive chord in the heart of every marriage proposal fan who saw it. The question which still haunts them, however, is, would Maureen O'Hara have made the same proposal if she had known what was going to happen to Edmond O'Brien in *D.O.A.*?

———————

Dirty Rotten Scoundrels (1988). That marriage proposal enthusiasts continue to have a strange way of going about select-

111

ing scenes for this genre is evidenced by their decision to include Michael Caine's proposal to the American widow as one of their choices. To begin with, it breaks one of their cardinal rules: That a marriage proposal scene should contain a proposal that is sincere. Even though Sydney Greenstreet's motives were mercenary, his proposal in *Three Strangers* was at least sincere. No, Caine didn't want to marry the widow. A movie audience would have to be pretty slow on the uptake to believe he wanted her to accept his offer of marriage after telling her that Steve Martin would also be sleeping in their marriage bed.

The Graduate (1967). Is it possible to get a proposal of marriage while you are at the altar getting married to another man? Yes, reports Katherine Ross, who got one just like that from Dustin Hoffman during the wacky dénouement of this very popular release directed by Mike Nichols. All Hoffman had to do was shout her name, whisk her out of the church and get her onto the back of a bus. To answer the many fans who have wondered if a marriage with that kind of beginning could work out, the answer is no. Ross was spotted out West two years later, first as a school teacher and then when she took up with Butch Cassidy and the Sundance Kid.

MEMORY

B E S T　　S C E N E S

The Treasure of the Sierra Madre (1948). Alfonso Bedoya is the victim of a Mexican boy's good memory in this John Huston masterpiece. Though few memory scene fans have shown much interest in the first two hours of this classic tale of greed and memory, all snap to attention during the final five minutes. That's when the little Mexican boy lifts the saddle cloths of the mules Bedoya was trying to sell. It's a thrilling moment. If the kid hadn't remembered they were the same mules he sold to the late Fred C. Dobbs, Bedoya would still be alive today. But he always remembers. Memory scene fans, not known for their sensitivity to the fate of Mexican bandits, would have it no other way.

Gigi (1958). It is quite unique. A song about memory in an award winning memory scene. When Hermione Gingold and Maurice Chevalier sing the captivating Lerner and Loewe classic, "I Remember It Well," memory scene fans were so charmed they made it the permanent theme song of their annual memory scene fan club dinner dance. Members meet for the black tie affair each year promptly at nine (or is it eight?). They are always on time (though many are late?). A tenor sings (or is it a baritone?). Are they getting old? Oh, no, not them! Ah yes, they remember it well.

Bogart remembers the Germans wore grey and Ingrid Bergman wore blue in *Casablanca* (1942).

Casablanca (1942). Everyone has their favorite moment in this very satisfying and still fresh classic. Mine is the way Conrad Veidt pronounces "dossier" while eating caviar as he tells Humphrey Bogart that he knows all about him. Memory scene fans probably don't even remember that scene. What they do remember, though, is how Bogart remembered that the Germans wore gray and Ingrid Bergman wore blue the last time he saw her and how Dooley Wilson finally remembers how to play "As Time Goes By," when Bergman asks him to: "Play it for me."

The 39 Steps (1935). Even as a young director, Alfred Hitchcock knew where to begin and end his films. The result is a pair of memory scenes that memory scene fans rank as "unforgettable." This unusually high assessment is due to a character in the film called Mr. Memory, who is, indeed, "One of the most remarkable men in the world."

In the opening scene Mr. Memory answers a number of pretty good questions, including a rather dull one from Robert Donat about how far Winnipeg is from Montreal. Donat's question in the final scene is not quite so dull. About to be arrested, he asks Mr. Memory, "What are the 39 steps?" Mr. Memory gets as far as saying, "The 39 steps are a secret organization of spies in the British government. . ." when a shot rings out and kills the poor man. But he doesn't die until he clears Donat by revealing the secret plans he had memorized.

One interesting sidelight to this film is that it contains a scene that may be the first time a scream turns into a train whistle. It occurs when Donat's landlady discovers the body of the murdered spy in his flat. In the middle of her scream, Hitchcock cuts to the Flying Scotsman speeding to Scotland, its whistle blaring. (This information is printed with the permission of the train-scene fan club, whose president shamefacedly admits that he lost the rights to this scene when he bet into a one card draw at the weekly memory scene fan club poker game.)

Field of Dreams (1989). There are more memory scenes in this movie than any ten movies in recent memory. One of the most amazing is pulled off by Burt Lancaster. Playing a small town doctor who gets his wish to go back in time and get his turn to bat in the big leagues, Lancaster is able to remember he is going to be a doctor when he grows up. This allows him to save the life of Kevin Costner's daughter when she swallows her hot dog. To a memory scene fan, future memories like this one are worth noting.

Also worth noting is Costner remembering that he never had that catch with his father when he was 14, and Lancaster remembering to wink at the pitcher when he gets his time at bat in the majors. A very beautiful movie and one that memory scene fans find especially satisfying.

Citizen Kane (1941). No, Everett Sloane didn't remember who or what "Rosebud" was, but he did remember a girl he saw on a ferry 50 years ago. "She was wearing a white dress. I only saw her for a few seconds. She didn't see me at all," Sloane tells the reporter. "Yet, I'll bet there hasn't been a day when I haven't thought about that girl," he adds wistfully.

Sloane's extraordinary feat of memory, added to the fact that he was still in love with the girl in the white dress, weighed heavily with memory scene fans. It is not a scene one can easily forget, and few seeing this film gem fail to share Sloane's regret at not meeting the girl, which is another reason memory scene fans decided to confer yet another movie scene award to this extraordinary, still fresh Orson Welles masterpiece.

Letter from an Unknown Woman (1948). It is not Louis Jourdan but his mute manservant who remembers Jourdan's affair with Joan Fontaine. Jourdan, now a dissolute concert pianist, has been up all night reading the letter which makes him realize how much Fontaine loved him and how she bore him a son and how they both died of fever. He learns all this on the morning he is to fight a duel with a jealous husband whose wife he has been having an affair with.

Memory scene fans, who never stay past the moment Jourdan remembers who Joan Fontaine is, voted the scene into memory scene history not knowing whether Jourdan survives the duel. Not being a memory scene fan myself, I have seen the ending and would like to inform them that he does not.

116

MIRROR

B E S T   S C E N E S

Ruthless (1945). The mirror scene in this nearly forgotten mirror masterpiece is a longtime favorite of mirror scene fans. The mirror is used for one reason and one reason only – to let Sydney Greenstreet know that his beautiful wife doesn't love him. Greenstreet is a good sport about it all. When his wife pushes him in front of their cheval glass and tells him in a very nasty manner, "You want to know why I don't love you? Look! Look at yourself," he just looks at his reflection and laughs, "A-heh. . . a-heh. . . a-heh-heh-heh." It is a particularly Greenstreetian laugh and the director gets the most out of the scene by shooting Greenstreet's reflection in the mirror at an up angle from the floor.

Taxi Driver (1976). Robert De Niro's masterful portrayal of a man who thinks his mirror is talking to him won out over its closest rival, the Wicked Queen talking to her mirror (*Snow White and the Seven Dwarfs*, 1937) by one vote. Everyone was bitterly disappointed that both scenes could not be listed as the Mirror Scene Rule Book clearly states that when more than one mirror scene involves someone asking a question of a mirror, only one can be chosen. "Mirror, mirror on the wall, who's the fairest of them all?" was judged to be a better question than, "You talkin' to me?" but what finally tipped the scale in De Niro's favor was that he drew a gun on his mirror when it didn't answer him.

The mirror scene in this nearly forgotten mirror masterpiece,
Ruthless **(1945), is a favorite of mirror scene fans.**

The Shining (1980). When Danny takes his mother's lipstick
and writes "REDRUM" on the bedroom door one could palpably
feel the anticipation of mirror scene fans in the audience. The anticipation may have been caused by the fact that a surprising
number of them can read and write backwards. In an unguarded
moment, Zellermeyer once told me they have often bored their
friends at parties by showing off this skill. Boredom was not
Shelley Duvall's reaction when her son shows off his "mirror
writing" skills in this scary and eccentric Kubrick thriller. She
nearly jumps out of her skin. To be fair, with Jack Nicholson
downstairs getting nuttier by the minute, and seeing the word
"REDRUM" reflecting in the mirror, who could blame her?

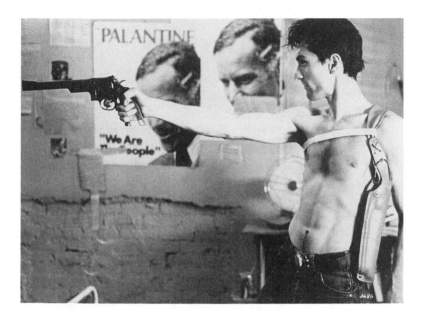

Robert De Niro drew a gun on his mirror when it didn't answer him in *Taxi Driver* (1976).

The Day of the Jackal (1973). A neat little mirror scene was inserted into this Fred Zinnermann winner just so France's President De Gaulle could see who was coming into his office. The sets were already in place. Zinnermann merely used the mirrored room of the presidential palace. So when the Minister of the Interior comes to see De Gaulle, De Gaulle's adjutant opens the door and announces him. That way, De Gaulle could see the minister's reflection in the mirror and know for sure it's really the minister coming to tell him about the assassination plot and not Edward Fox coming to carry it out.

Broadcast News (1987). The height at which Holly Hunter's mirror was placed on her apartment wall is a source of great amusement among mirror scene fans. Not known for their sense of humor, they surprised members of the D.O.A. at their triannual awards dinner by laughing during the presentation of the award for this winning selection.

When the scene in which Holly Hunter has to climb up on a chair in order to look at herself in the mirror for her date with William Hurt was shown on the monitor, a definite outbreak of giggling could be heard at the mirror scene fan club table. Their president, Bret Schlesinger, was positively droll when he suggested that the choice of a scene which lasted but five seconds was a good reflection on mirror scenes everywhere.

Dracula (1931). The brief, but sly mirror scene in this Bela Lugosi classic did not go unnoticed by mirror scene fans. The canny Van Helsing knew that Count Dracula would never walk into a room with a mirror prominently displayed, so he prepares a small box, which when opened, has a mirror on the inside. When Lugosi is safely inside the room, Van Helsing opens the box and looks into the mirror to see if Lugosi's reflection can be seen. Since vampires do not traditionally have a mirror reflection, he does not see Lugosi in the mirror.

When Van Helsing confronts Lugosi with the mirror, Bela knocks it out of his hand in a rare fit of vampire pique. Now Van Helsing knows for certain that Lugosi is a vampire, Lugosi knows that Van Helsing knows he is a vampire, and mirror scene fans know they can safely include a classic vampire mirror scene on their awards list.

Many film fans are under the assumption that the Mirror Scene Rule Book states a vampire mirror scene must be included in any list of awards. It does not. This film won its place on merit alone.

Big Business (1988). Mirror scene fans always look fondly on a movie that pays homage to one of their favorite scenes. So it was in this film about two sets of twins, one set who could imitate Groucho and Harpo Marx in *Duck Soup* (1933) and one set who couldn't. The two sets of twins are able to discover they were put in the wrong cribs at birth only when the Bette Midler twins succeed with the famous mirror routine in the ladies room, complete with the thumbing of the nose and sticking out of tongues. When the Lily Tomlin twins try they get so scared they can't do it. There is a funny line, not in the original routine, when Midler accuses the other two twins of being "pod people."

Mr. Skeffington (1944). Okay, before she went sailing in the rain and caught diphtheria and lost her looks and her hair, Bette Davis was so vain she could not pass a mirror without looking into it. And, yes, after Davis got diphtheria, the only time she would look into a mirror was by accident. All this, mirror scene fans find mildly interesting.

What really interests them is that by the time Davis had lost her looks and was wearing the wig and the pasty makeup, Claude Rains, who plays the title role, had lost his sight. Even better, since he had never seen her with the wig and the pasty makeup, he only remembers her as a beautiful woman. In mirror scene parlance, Rains had become the perfect mirror. Now every time Davis looks at him, and sees the love in his face, she will see herself as he "sees" her – a beautiful woman. Yes, the movie ends here, but many mirror scene fans think this was a big mistake. For them, this is where it really starts to get interesting.

All About Eve (1950). Supporting the theory that mirror scenes rarely bode anything good for anyone is the final dramatic moment is this nest-of-vipers classic. The scene in question is set up when Anne Baxter (Eve Harrington) returns to her apartment

121

to find the teenage president of the Eve Harrington fan club (Erasmus Hall branch) asleep in her apartment. It soon becomes obvious that the girl is going to do to Anne Baxter what Baxter did to Bette Davis.

When Baxter leaves the room, the young girl grabs Baxter's Tony award, drapes Baxter's fur stole around her shoulders and steps into the three-way mirror and bows. The scene is shot so one can see the mirror image of the girl holding Baxter's award into infinity. The image is so powerful that it is responsible for the coining of the phrase "mirror impact." Mirror scene fans do not usually reveal the mirror impact rating of their selections but word has it that this fadeout scene got a 10.

MODEL AIRPLANE

B E S T   S C E N E S

Empire of the Sun. (1987). "Give the kid back his plane," was the cry heard most at the model airplane scene club viewing of this Spielberg gem about a model airplane being separated from a boy who was separated from his parents for the entire length of the Second World War. The plane was the kid's glider which stays aloft an extraordinarily long time but finally lands in a Japanese army encampment. Causing the outcry is the fact that the Japanese soldiers refused to give it back to the boy, played wonderfully by Christian Bale. The glider was lost nearly four years until a young Japanese model airplane fan at the airfield near the boy's prison camp returns it.

Some model airplane scene intellectuals have even suggested both model plane scenes in this movie employed storytelling devices known as "foreshadowing." It was Spielberg's way of saying that the boy would be lost by his parents when he lost the plane and would be found again when he finds the plane. They may have been right. Right after the boy lost his plane, his parents lost him, and right after he found the plane, his parents found him again.

The Fallen Idol (1949). Although paper airplanes are not expressly mentioned in the Model Airplane Scene Book of Rules, neither are they expressly forbidden. This was the reasoning used to allow the scene in which the "dart," as Ralph Richardson calls the paper airplane Bobby Henrey made, to be considered in this category. The scene won its award not because the plane was constructed from paper on which a vital message from Ralph Richardson's mistress was written (like great cigar scenes, great model airplane scenes need have nothing to do with plot), but because, considering the paper model airplane was made by a ten-year-old, it flew remarkably well for an indoor flight.

The Flight of the Phoenix (1966). Any model airplane scene lover who ever wanted to fly in his or her model airplane can see his or her fantasy come true in this World War II film starring Jimmy Stewart and Hardy Kruger. But in order to get seven grown men into a model plane the story must first make sense. This it does. That's because the only way for them to get out of the desert before they die of thirst is to build a plane and the only one who knows how to build a plane is Hardy Kruger. The problem is the only kind of planes Kruger has ever built were model airplanes.

Model airplane scene fans still don't understand why the men lose faith in Kruger when they find this out. Didn't Kruger explain to them that a real airplane is just a model airplane, only bigger? He was right. Kruger builds the biggest model airplane in film history, the men lie down on the wings, and Jimmy Stewart gives them all a wild model airplane ride to safety.

Wargames (1983). Because the Model Airplane Scene Book of Rules contains no rule about what a model airplane should look like, model airplane scene fans have assumed that one could be built to resemble a pterodactyl. Purists of this genre do not agree and argue that the flying dinosaur Matthew Broderick saw on the island was not a model airplane that looked like a pterodactyl; it was a model pterodactyl. Less concerned about Broderick's attempt to stop the computer game "Global Thermonuclear Warfare" from becoming a reality, they threatened to resign from the genre and form their own model pterodactyl club if model airplane scene fans went ahead with their plans to call it a model airplane. When it was pointed out that model pterodactyl scenes might be hard to come by, they backed down from their threat, agreed to consider it a model airplane and voted the scene its award.

Easy Money (1983). Model airplane scenes are rare to begin with but one that includes the building of a Messerschmitt occur even more infrequently. Practically unique is one in which the actor building the Messerschmitt is Rodney Dangerfield. But it does exist and model airplane scene fans feel it is a classic. The path to Dangerfield's building a model airplane isn't hard to follow. To inherit $10 million he must stop gambling, drinking and womanizing. But it isn't easy so his wife tells him to get a hobby. The hobby he chooses is model airplanes, very gratifying to model airplane scene fans but hard on Dangerfield. For one thing, he has to build it in the house, which means he has to listen to his daughter practice the violin. For another, he'd rather be at the racetrack.

When his friend suggests taking a look at the department store he is going to inherit, he jumps at the chance to leave the house. But not before delivering one of the greatest model airplane scene lines in film history. As he passes his wife he remarks, "There's a Messerschmitt in the kitchen. Clean it up, will ya?"

Model Airplane Movie — Title Not Remembered (circa 1942). The model airplane scene in this film was considered so extraordinary it won its listing despite the fact that no model airplane scene fan could remember the film's title, could name the actor who played the lead, or knew the year it was made. What they are certain of is an army private's ingenious use of model airplanes. He uses them to teach recruits rifle marksmanship by flying the model airplanes toward them on the firing line. The soldiers use them as moving targets and try to shoot them down.

When the crabby sergeant (whose name no one could remember, either) complains to the commanding officer, he is put on the firing line, given a rifle, and told to try it himself. Much to the delight of model airplane fans, he misses the planes which crash into him one by one. Model airplane hobbyists (of which there are many in model airplane scene fan clubs) did have one reservation about the film. They were uncertain if model airplanes with propellers powered by rubberbands could fly in such a straight path. But when faced with a model airplane scene that gave so much pleasure, they did not make a big issue of it.

Dead Poet's Society (1989). When is a flying desk set a model airplane and when is it a desk set? That question was answered definitively by the model airplane scene fan club when they voted it this award. Their decision to consider it a model airplane was subsequently approved by the D.O.A., which gave this precedent-setting explanation for its action: (1) When the desk set was first seen, its aerodynamic design was noted. (2) It was referred to as a "flying desk set" and subsequently thrown from the roof. (3) Though the birthday gift was given to a teenager as a desk set, it was the same desk set he got on his previous birthday. Since the young man was a member of a group that encouraged its members to look at things differently, he has every right to call it anything he wanted. Since he chose to call it a flying desk set, it was considered fair game for model airplane scene fans.

Model airplane scene fans are devastated over the absence of the "flying brain stretcher" that flew around Val Kilmer's dormitory room in *Real Genius* (1985). They felt that a word of explanation was in order about the decision to leave it off the list. Needless to say, the discussion about whether a radio controlled flying space probe lookalike can be called an "airplane" became quite heated. In the end, a large majority of the members felt that if the "flying brain stretcher" scene were to be included on the list, it would make model airplane fans appear so hungry for model airplane scenes that they would consider anything that flew as a possibility. Besides, the object in question didn't even have wings!

It should also be noted that there were some model airplane scene enthusiasts who insisted that the plane to Lisbon in *Casablanca* was a model airplane. They were prevailed upon by cooler heads not to persist in this hypothesis. If that can of worms were to be opened up, practically every movie made in the 1930s and early 1940s would have had to be considered.

NAME MISPRONUNCIATION

B E S T   S C E N E S

Gentleman's Agreement (1947). Only Gregory Peck has the stature to pull off the ultimate name mispronunciation in film history and get away from it. Throughout the entire length of this Elia Kazan Oscar-winner, Peck calls his mother (Ann Revere) "Maw." Not once does he call her "Ma," or "Mom," or even "Mother." The fact that Ann Revere never once corrects him is proof of the unselfishness of a mother's love.

The Third Man (1950). In this film about a man interrupted from carving roast beef to get his name mispronounced, Joseph Cotten mispronounces Doctor Winkle's name with such innocence the audience never knows whether he does it on purpose or not. When Winkle is called out from the dining room, Cotten's words, "Dr. Winkle?" and Dr. Winkle's controlled response *"Vin...*kle" sends a shiver up the spine of name mispronunciation fans across the country. During the scene, which lasts but a moment, Cotten keeps calling Winkle "Winkle," and Winkle keeps correcting him with, *"Vin...*kel!" The scene is so charged that it becomes difficult for the audience to remember why Cotten had gone there in the first place.

Chinatown (1974). Rarely is there a film where name mispronunciation was so preventable as is the case in this Roman Polanski film noir. When John Huston keeps calling Jack Nicholson "Getts" instead of "Geddes," it soon becomes obvious he never saw *Citizen Kane*. Nicholson could have prevented all this by taking Huston to a showing of "Kane" and have him watch the scene where Welles (Kane) is denouncing his political opponent, "Boss Jim Geddes." Welles pronounces "Gedd-es" so clearly that Huston would certainly have gotten it right the next time he had to say it. In fact, Welles pronounced it so well in *Citizen Kane* that Geddes got mad and tattled to the press about Welles's affair with Dorothy Comingore, which costs Welles the election. But that's another film.

Touch of Evil (1958). Given the chance, few actors could ever pronounce the name "Vargas" the way Akim Tamiroff does. In the scene where he is upset at the young punk for throwing acid at Charlton Heston, he grabs the punk by the lapel, shouting, "Who tol' you to throw acid at Whargus!" Yes, Tamiroff has had trouble with his "V"s in a number of films, but coming up with "Whargus," while wearing an ill-fitting wig that keeps falling off, so enraptured name mispronunciation fans that they voted the film into the award category.

Brazil (1985). The only known instance of computer name mispronunciation takes place in this Terry Gilliam film in which a computer that meant to say "Tuttle" says "Buttle." Apparently, computer name mispronunciation in films is quite serious. Buttle winds up dead. Tuttle sticks around for the entire film fixing things. Some name mispronunciation buffs think this was because Tuttle was played by Robert De Niro.

Rain Man (1988) Name mispronunciation fans are particu-

130

larly fond of this movie starring Dustin Hoffman and Tom Cruise because of its delayed fuse. It isn't until the film is halfway over that we discover when Cruise was saying "Rain Man" as a two-year-old, he was trying to say, "Raymond." Particularly appreciated is the fact that Hoffman knew this all the time but didn't let on.

***

The Laughing Policeman (1973). Walter Matthau is not only a good detective, his ability to correctly figure out a suspect's name even though it is unbelievably butchered earns him the affection of name mispronunciation fans everywhere. When he and Bruce Dern are trying to get the name of a possible bus killer from one of Matthau's unsavory sources in that coffee shop, the only name the stoolie can come up with is "Rah-Denny." It would take a pretty hardnosed name mispronunciation fan not to be thrilled when Matthau translates "Rah-Denny" into "Rodney." The fact that it was a false lead in no way bars this scene from its place of honor.

***

Bus Stop (1956). Even admirers of name mispronunciation scenes have been known to wince when Don Murray keeps calling Marilyn Monroe "Cherry" even after she repeatedly tells him her name is "Cher-ie." Monroe takes it with good grace, though, and Murray finally gets it right after four or five attempts.

***

Suspicion (1941). After searching through the Name Mispronunciation Scene Book of Rules in a frantic effort to allow the scenes in which Cary Grant refers to Joan Fontaine as "Monkey Face" to receive a name mispronunciation award, the attempt was abandoned. Though the rules give a lot of leeway to what is considered a name mispronunciation, there was no getting around Rule 6. Rule 6 states, "Except in the case of where a 'v' is pronounced as a 'w' [as in *Touch of Evil* and *The Third Man*], a name mispronunciation must begin with the same letter as the person's name to be considered as such." Since the character played by Joan Fontaine is named "Lena," and "monkey face" clearly begins with an "m" and not an "l," it could not legally be considered a name mispronunciation and remains what it clearly was intended to be, a cruel term of endearment. Many name mispronunciation psychologists feel the choice of such an unkind nickname for Miss Fontaine was Hitchcock's way of getting her to remain so stiff and self-conscious throughout the film.

NECK BRACE

B E S T   S C E N E S

Grand Illusion (1938). The story is well known in neck brace circles, and it is true. Erich von Stroheim's neck brace was not a result of a World War I injury. The idea was his own. Von Stroheim just appeared on the set one day wearing one. His neck brace diary revealed that he was searching for a way to make the prison camp commandant more interesting and decided that a neck brace was the way to go. It was an inspired idea, for the vintage classic truly comes alive in every scene von Stroheim appears.

Best moment: When von Stroheim has to shoot Pierre Fresnay, the French nobleman who had been his prisoner and friend. No doubt von Stroheim was aiming for the leg as he claims, and a pistol shot at 150 feet is certainly a difficult shot, as the mortally wounded Fresnay says. But, in private, von Stroheim has always indicated that if he had not been wearing the damned neck brace, he would have made the shot.

Funny Farm (1988). What finally won the neck brace scene in this loony but likeable Chevy Chase film its award was the fact that it contains one of the funniest neck brace lines in recent memory. A lawyer, wearing a neck brace that tilts his head up, says to the lawyer in whose office he is sitting, "You ought to get this ceiling painted once in a while." Neck brace scene fans, not accustomed to humor from lawyers, especially about neck braces,

Von Stroheim always said that if he had not been wearing the damned neck brace, he would have made the shot in *Grand Illusion* (1938).

do not think this very funny throwaway line will be topped for a long time to come.

———————

Five Easy Pieces (1970). Perhaps it was to prove that people who wear neck braces could lead active lives that led Ralph Waite to play that vicious game of Ping-Pong with Jack Nicholson. Was Nicholson too hard on Waite when he beat him 21 to 2? Neck brace scene fans are divided on this question. Those that say Nicholson was too hard on his injured brother (Waite) don't buy the argument that if he had gone easier it would have been a form of condescension.

134

Neck brace medical experts point out that a score of 21 to 2 is not that unusual when someone with a neck injury plays Ping-Pong with someone whose neck is not injured. Neck brace psychologists in this group add that the game was also a clever and visual way to show how Nicholson felt about his brother. All agree that it is a superb neck brace scene, probably the only one extant in which an actor wearing one plays Ping-Pong. Favorite line: Waite, wearing his neck brace, says to Nicholson, "I'm not sure you know of my accident."

ORCHESTRA

B E S T   S C E N E S

The Red Shoes (1948). Though Moira Shearer is indeed lovely in her movie debut, it is Marius Goring who holds the main interest of orchestra scene fans. Goring, a young composer, is first spotted in the balcony watching his music teacher conduct a score for a ballet supposedly written by the teacher. He quickly discovers that it is his own music and that his music teacher had stolen it from him. When we next see Goring, he is the orchestra coach of Anton Walbrook's ballet company. Goring has called an extra rehearsal because he doesn't like the way his piece is being played. Orchestra scene fans feel it was worth paying the orchestra overtime since it resulted in one of the great orchestra scene lines in movie history. When Goring asks one of the musicians, "Do you have a B-flat there?" and the musician answers, "no," Goring responds with, "Ah, that makes all the difference, doesn't it?"

This scene is also important because it results in Walbrook's commissioning Goring to write a new score for the ballet, *The Red Shoes*. This leads up to a moment that orchestra scene fans hold very dear – Goring, at the podium, ready to conduct his music, deliberately closing the scorebook and lifting his baton. He is going to conduct his piece without looking at the music!

There are many diehard orchestra scene fans who have privately admitted to having never seen Moira Shearer dance in *The Red Shoes*, because the camera never goes back to Goring at the podium and they felt no reason to stick around any longer.

100 Men and a Girl (1937). Probably the only orchestra ever to play in a lobby is the one Adolphe Menjou got together made up of unemployed musicians. Menjou's daughter, played by Deanna Durbin, tries to get Leopold Stokowski to conduct. It's the only way they can get a job on radio. (Remember this was 1937.) Durbin leads the great conductor into this huge lobby.

Suddenly, we hear music. Musicians begin to appear on the balcony and from every corner of the place. They are playing their hearts out. The music is so arousing, so seductive that Stokowski can't resist. He begins to conduct. There he is, standing in the middle of a lobby, looking up to the balcony for the horns, into a corner for the strings as he conducts his heart away. It is such a musically satisfying and witty scene that it won over the hearts of orchestra scene fans everywhere.

———

The Competition (1980). When Amy Irving's piano goes out of tune while she was "piano-faking" the Mozart, it was a tough break for Mozart fans but a lucky one for Prokofiev lovers. Lucky, too, were orchestra scene fans with a sense of humor. When Sam Wanamaker complains that he might not be in the mood to play the Prokofiev, Lee Remick, Irving's piano teacher delivers one of the funniest orchestra lines orchestra scene fans can remember hearing. She storms up to Wanamaker and tells him that, "It costs extra to carve 'schmuck' on a tombstone. But you would definitely be worth the expense!" Wanamaker has the grace to laugh, Irving gets a chance to play the Prokofiev, and Remick endeared herself to orchestra scene fans for all time.

———

The Man Who Knew Too Much (1956). Alfred Hitchcock is no friend of orchestra scene fans. He promises us a thrilling orchestra scene in the opening credits and then makes us wait until the movie is practically over before delivering. Happily, orchestra scene fans who do wait are rewarded with a pretty good one.

By this time they know that when the orchestra gets to the part when the cymbals crash, the prime minister of a foreign country will be assassinated. They also know that Doris Day's son is in the hands of the assassins. Hitchcock, mischievous as ever, makes Day choose between saving her son and listening to an awful piece of music called the "Storm Cloud Sonata." She chooses the music, leaving it up to Jimmy Stewart to stop the assassin.

Here, Hitchcock begins to deliver on his promise and give us the sequence of orchestra scenes that orchestra fans were waiting for: The pan shot of the orchestra including a chorus which must number over five hundred women; the cymbals, each resting on its own chair; the assassin, hiding behind a curtain; the prime minister in his box (he actually seems to be enjoying the music); Day, looking frantically from the assassin's box to the prime minister's box; Stewart, rushing madly around Albert Hall trying to find the assassin's box; the assassin's assistant following the score; the cymbalist picking up the cymbals and getting ready; the assassin's gun, sticking out from behind the curtain; the cymbals finally clashing; Day finally screaming; the gun finally firing; the prime minster finally getting shot (in the arm); Stewart finally wrestling with the assassin; and the assassin finally falling from the balcony.

It should be mentioned (finally) that Hitchcock's secret orchestra scene diary revealed that the reason he chose such awful music was that he knew that a decent piece would have been too distracting. What the diary does not explain is why he needed a five hundred woman chorus or how the prime minister could possibly enjoy such music.

———

Named on the first string team of actors who knew their way around a good violin concerto were John Garfield for choosing his violin over Joan Crawford in *Humoresque* (1946); Vittorio Gassman for chosing his violin over Elizabeth Taylor in *Rhapsody*

(1954); and Stewart Granger for his masterful portrayal of Niccolò Paganini in *The Magic Bow* (1947), a movie whose title few orchestra scene fans can remember: What they do remember is the scene in which Granger is playing one of Paganini's violin concertos during a concert in Vienna at a time when Napoleon's troops are about to capture the city. During his performance the concert hall doors swing open, troops surround the audience, and a French general marches down the aisle. But Granger's fiddling so charms the general that he allows the concert to continue and marches back up the aisle in step to Paganini's music and Granger's violin.

PARKING METER

BEST SCENES

Playtime (1967). Only the incomparable Jacques Tati could find joy in something that was designed to make man so nervous. Tati saves his memorable parking meter moment for the final scene of this film. To set it up, he first gives us a shot of a Parisian traffic circle crowded with cars, trucks and tour buses going slowly round and round and round to the music of a carousel. Suddenly, the traffic and music stop.

Into camera range walks Tati, who instantly sizes up the situation and does something which underscores his unique parking meter sensibility. He puts a coin in a parking meter. The moment he does this, the traffic and carousel music start up again. Tati then walks off as if putting a coin in a parking meter to start up traffic again is the most natural occurrence in the world. This is not only a brilliant and original use of a parking meter, it is a genuinely funny and fresh scene. Many parking meter fans feel that if Tati is to be remembered for just one screen moment, this should be it.

Cool Hand Luke (1967). One reason there have been so few parking meter scenes to choose from may be due to this Warner Bros. release. When Paul Newman saws off the tops of those parking meters, he nearly exhausts the parking meter population in Hollywood. Few parking meter scene devotees can watch this scene without mixed feelings. They appreciate the scene's unique qualities, but at the same time understand that it had two grave consequences: It resulted in Newman's being sent to the prison where he was shot by the guard who always wore sunglasses, and Newman's wanton destruction of those parking meters resulted in the filming of only two parking meter scenes since.

━━━━━━━━━━

Bananas (1971). A direct result of the parking meter shortage caused by Paul Newman in *Cool Hand Luke* four years before is the parking meter scene in this Woody Allen release which had to be shot without a parking meter. In Allen's now famous dream sequence, four monks carrying a large wooden cross upon which Woody Allen is tied start backing into a parking space. Another four monks carrying a large wooden cross to which someone else is tied start to park their cross in the same parking space and a fist fight breaks out.

Allen's secret notes for the film revealed that he intended to have the winning monks park the cross and deposit a coin in a parking meter. But no meter could be found in Hollywood and it was written out of the scene. It might be interesting to note here that until Allen's notes for the dream sequence were found, this scene was thought to be an alternate-side-of-the-street parking scene.

PRISON

B E S T S C E N E S

White Heat (1949). One needn't be a great fan of prison scenes to recognize a great prison scene. Probably the best of this genre, and certainly the most carefully choreographed, is that memorable moment when Jimmy Cagney finds out his mother is dead. First, Cagney spots a new prisoner seated about six prisoners away from where he is eating. Then, he whispers to the prisoner next to him to find out from the new prisoner how his mother is doing.

The message is passed along (in whispers) from inmate to inmate until the new prisoner gets it. He then passes back the answer, from inmate to inmate, until the prisoner next to Cagney says in a stage whisper, "She's dead." This is the moment Cagney, who has always been something of a Momma's boy, was waiting for. His reaction is known and loved by prison scene fans all over the world.

First, Cagney starts to whine; then he bangs his head on the table; then he climbs on the table and starts to crawl over everybody's lunch. When the guards try to stop him, he punches three of them out until he is finally subdued. Proof of the high regard in which this scene is held is the D.O.A.'s speed squashing of a food-mushing fan bid to place this scene in their category. A spokesman for the D.O.A. had this to say about the food-mushing change of venue request: "Calling the Jimmy Cagney lunchroom scene a food-mushing scene would be like calling *Treasure of the*

143

One needn't be a fan of prison scenes to recognize a great one— *White Heat* (1949).

Sierra Madre a movie about bad haircuts." An apology was made to haircut scene fans who took offense at this analogy and the matter was dropped.

Kind Hearts and Coronets (1950). This highly gratifying British film, which has everything–love, greed, ambition, a balloon ascension and Alec Guinness playing eight roles–also has a neat little prison scene. Dennis Price, who has murdered Guinness eight times so he could inherit the title and name of Gascoyne-Dascoyne, is in prison charged with a murder he did not commit. He spends the time in prison writing in his diary about how he murdered all the Gascoyne-Dascoynes who were ahead of him in line for the title.

When it is finally proved that Price is innocent of the crime for which he has been charged, he walks out of the prison, only to realize he has left his diary in his cell. Though prison scene fans frown on prison scenes that have anything to do with the dénouement of a film, Price's elegant prison manners and the final shot of his diary in the cell being read by the prison guards packed enough wallop to sway the vote in his favor.

Angels with Dirty Faces (1938). Few prison scene admirers will ever forgive Pat O'Brien for asking James Cagney to pretend to be afraid when they marched him off to the electric chair so the Dead End Kids wouldn't think a killer was a hero. Cagney, a veteran of many prison movies, took it all in good grace. He breaks down on his last walk to the "chair" but never lets on whether he did it because O'Brien asked him to, or because he was really afraid. In the end, it was Cagney's effortless prison deportment that gave him a second prison laurel and earned this scene its award.

Take the Money and Run (1969). When Woody Allen vows that he will never serve out his full term, prison scene fans know they are in for a special treat. They are not disappointed. Allen first gives them a prison escape in which the character he plays fashions a gun from a bar of soap and shoe polish. If it wasn't raining, the escape would have been successful. Unfortunately, the guards became suspicious when the gun turned to soap bubbles.

Allen's second attempt to leave prison early was less ingenious, but more successful. It led to a parole. To get the parole, he volunteers to test a new vaccine. The vaccine had only one side effect. For several hours Allen is turned into a rabbi (a prison first). These scenes alone are enough to satisfy even the most demanding prison scene enthusiast, but Allen isn't through. He has one great prison scene left. It is the classic escape after he is sent back to prison for a second term.

The escape works, but there were problems. When nobody tells him that the break was called off, Allen finds himself in the prison courtyard being laughed at by his fellow inmates. Allen, remarkably resourceful, has the last laugh. He takes a cab and makes his escape. Prison fans were particularly pleased with "Virgil Starkwell" as Allen's choice of name for the character he played. On a prisoner name authenticity scale of one to ten, it rated a 9.8, with "Al Capone" the only prisoner name to receive a higher rating.

=========

The sudden lack of a quorum due to parole violations by two members of the prison scene fan club curtailed any further voting. Among the films that were up for an award were: *I Want to Live* (1958), starring Susan Hayward; *Brute Force* (1947), starring Hume Cronyn and Burt Lancaster; *Birdman of Alcatraz* (1962), starring Burt Lancaster and Karl Malden; *Calling Northside 777* (1948), starring James Stewart; and *20,000 Years in Sing Sing* (1933), starring Spencer Tracy and Bette Davis. Because this lack of a quorum has happened on more than one occasion, the Prison Scene Fan Club Rules Committee recently decided to accept write-in ballots.

SAGGING SHOULDERS

BEST SCENES

Breaking the Sound Barrier (1947). Many have heard the rumors: Ralph Richardson improvised the scene; the director was afraid to attempt it even though it was in the shooting script; Richardson had done the scene 21 times and was simply tired. Whichever is true, the sagging shoulders scene in this British film stands so far above all others in the category that sagging shoulders scene fans closed the voting after its selection.

The great moment occurs as Denholm Elliot, Richardson's son, crashes his Spitfire while trying to land during his first solo flight. At the moment of impact, Richardson, who had been watching the flight with his back to the camera, allows his shoulders to sag with such expression that the audience knows instantly he really loved his son despite the fact that he was a lousy pilot. They also know that Richardson is sorry for forcing him to take flying lessons even though he knew Elliot hated flying.

To be sure, there are other sagging shoulders scenes that were up for an award. One desperate clique of sagging shoulders scene fans insisted that Marlon Brando's sagging shoulders scene after his defeat in the battle of Waterloo in *Desiree* (1954) be included. Another group was in favor of giving Oscar Humulka's slumping shoulders reaction in *War and Peace* (1956) an award. But the majority of sagging shoulders scene fans held firm. Their argument was hard to refute: a good sagging shoulders scene is not a great sagging shoulders scene.

When informed that they might lose their accreditation with the D.O.A. because of the paucity of their selections (one scene in five years), the members of the sagging shoulders scene fan club agreed to give up something they cherished nearly as much as sagging shoulders scenes – their recipe for the perfect medium boiled egg. The offer was accepted and this amazingly simple way to make a perfect medium boiled egg is revealed here for the first time.

THE PERFECT MEDIUM BOILED EGG

Fill a pot with water. Place into it two eggs. Light the burner. When the water starts to boil, put a slice of bread into the automatic toaster. When the toast pops up, remove the eggs from the pot and serve. (Author's note: I have tried this recipe many times, and it has not failed me once.)

SHADOW

B E S T   S C E N E S

The untimely breakup of the shadow scene fan club, caused by the inability of a single member to name the movie in which Goliath cast his giant shadow over David, unfortunately took place before the members were scheduled to vote on their selections. A chance meeting with the former scribe of the defunct organization enabled me to obtain a copy of his notes, which contain a partial listing of some of the scenes the former members were considering. I was given permission to make them public after promising to make no changes. They are recreated on these pages verbatim.

The Gay Divorcee (1934). Ingenious idea...paper cutouts on a record player turntable. Lampshade. Spinning round and round making shadow on wall that looks like two people dancing...allows Fred Astaire and Ginger Rogers to sneak out while everyone thinks they're up there dancing. Find out name of tune. Is it "Continental" or "Night and Day"? Check if there is a record player fan club. Will there be any trouble with them on this?

Citizen Kane (1941). Check with D.O.A. to see if any other club is considering this movie for award. Did Comingore really think Welles making his finger look like a rooster shadow was funny?

The Magnificent Ambersons (1942). Welles again! This time responsible for putting Joseph Cotten's shadow on door of dead father's room and telling him to walk closer so shadow will loom bigger and bigger.

———————

The Third Man (1949). Check with lawyer on status of restraining order re: balloon vendor shadow. Is it ours or not?

———————

The Letter (1940). Set up screening. Find out if clouds passing over moon obscuring Gale Sondergaard's face count as shadows, if affirmative, put spelling of Sondergaard name on admissions test to club...

———————

Except for a personal note to check the TV listing for the time that *Shadow of the Thin Man* (circa 1940) goes on, this was the final entry.

SPIDER

B E S T   S C E N E S

Annie Hall (1977). When Diane Keaton calls Woody Allen up in the middle of the night and asks him to come over to kill the spider in her bathtub, spider scene fans know they are in for a treat. Allen doesn't let them down. Yes, he asks for a can of Raid first, admittedly a poor start, but he redeems himself by doing the job with a tennis racket. He nearly achieves spider scene perfection by popping out of the bathroom every few seconds to inform Keaton of his progress and informing her that it is not one spider he is dealing with but two.

Zellermeyer, in his capacity as D.O.A. recording secretary, was present at the vote. He has this footnote to add: When one of the members wanted to discuss how it must have felt to be Shelley Duvall, the actress Allen left behind when he went over to Keaton's apartment, she was stripped of her membership and her subscription to *Spider Scene Quarterly* was cancelled on the spot.

Dr. No (1963). Though it is true the 007 designation gives James Bond the license to kill spiders, many film fans have asked themselves whether 19 blows with a shoe wasn't somewhat excessive. That is one of the questions spider scene fans had to deal with before deciding whether this scene was consigned to oblivion or marked for film history. The fact that Sean Connery, who plays

151

Allen doesn't know it yet, but this is the tennis racket he will kill the spider with in Diane Keaton's bathtub in *Annie Hall* (1977).

Bond, was sick in the bathroom after the spider squashing, is reported to have had some affect on the voting.

To be fair, some spider scene fans feel this was a normal reaction to a tarantula crawling up his body while he slept. Unfortunately, this argument only led to another question: "Why was the spider covered up by a sheet through so much of the scene?" The tarantula scene subcommittee of organized spider scene fans are surprisingly reticent about revealing their true feelings about this scene, saying simply that its presence in this book speaks for itself.

The Thief of Bagdad (1940). A favorite entertainment at

spider scene get-togethers is to ask first-time guests what was the first line to the song that Sabu sings when he climbs the giant spider web. It's a good question, one that no true spider scene fan would ever fail to answer. The line, of course, is: "I want to be a sailor, sailing out to sea." Some film fans may regard this type of amusement as unusual, but then spider scene fans have always been considered a bit strange. A lot of this may have to do with their inability to resolve their love-hate relationship with spiders. They hate spiders but they love film scenes with spiders. These dual feelings are best illustrated in the choice of this scene.

Spider scene fans admit the giant spider gets less frightening with each viewing but voted for it because Sabu kills it. It has been said that analysts, upon discovering they have a spider scene fan as a client, often have a difficult time restraining themselves from shouting "Yippee!" during the session.

The Fly (1958). So accustomed are spider scene fans to seeing spiders get killed, they no longer shush David Hedison when he is crying, "Help me," after he gets caught in the spider's web. Nor do spider scene fans blame themselves when the spider (and Hedison) are crushed by the policeman in the final scene. To be completely accurate, it is not quite all of Hedison that is caught in the web, just his head and one of his arms.

Spider scene fans love spider scenes so much they can be excused for overlooking the fact that the web and the spider in this film look as if they are more likely to be seen in a rain forest than in a private home. It is a powerful scene nevertheless and keeps intact their record of never awarding a spider scene in which a spider doesn't get killed.

The Incredible Shrinking Man (1957). Another spider bites the dust in this original (and best) version of the film when Grant Williams stabs it with a sewing needle. The argument between Williams and the spider was over a crumb of bread. The spider needed it in order to live and keep growing. Williams needed it in order to live and keep shrinking. Since there obviously wasn't enough food in the cellar for both a spider and a shrinking man, there was no objection raised by the authorities when it was discovered that the spider was killed with an unregistered sewing needle.

Dracula (1931). It somehow seems fitting that the one spider to survive a spider scene lives in Castle Dracula. Bela Lugosi puts it eloquently when he observes, "The spider spinning its web for the unwitting fly. The blood is delight." Spider scene fans still wonder how Lugosi got through the spider web without breaking it. Renfield, who was following only a few steps behind, practically had to chop his way through it. Spider scene fans see only two possible answers to this question, which has puzzled them for more than decades. Either vampires can walk through spider webs without breaking them, or the spiders in Castle Dracula are unusually nimble when it comes to spinning webs.

STEAMBATH

BEST SCENES

T-Men (1947). Nearly every afternoon at 2:17 P.M. a member of the steambath scene fan club, carrying a bag of Chinese litchi nuts, walks into the steamroom. A minute later, two other members lock him in and turn up the steam. The member inside bangs on the door, puts his face up to the glass window and shouts for them to let him out. At this point all the members of the club who are present gather in the steamroom area and chant, "Schemer, Schemer, Schemer," before they let him out.

This ritual is in honor of Wallace Ford, the actor who played "Schemer," the character in this film who was murdered by being steamed to death in his favorite steamroom. Many steambath fans consider it to be the greatest steambath scene ever filmed. Steambath scene fans now believe they have pinpointed the precise time of day "Schemer" was murdered and like to recreate the crime each afternoon when there is a quorum present at the club.

Gorky Park (1983). One might not think that steambath scene fans are particularly sensitive to beauty, but they are. Many consider the Moscow (Helsinki, actually) steamroom in this movie to be among the most beautiful they have ever seen. A balcony surrounds a huge pool. There are private rooms where one can rest after a steam. Tables of caviar and blini are set up

155

everywhere so members can eat well while they replace the body's need for salt. So beautiful is the place that when a sliver of food escapes onto William Hurt's upper lip it so mars the splendor of this steamroom that Lee Marvin feels compelled to make Hurt aware of it with the words, "Man overboard."

Spartacus (1960). Steambath scene fans have long been accused of turning to ancient Rome whenever they needed a good steambath scene and this choice is often cited as proof of that accusation. This is vigorously denied by steambath scene legalists who point out that the steambath scene between Charles Laughton and Laurence Olivier stands on its own. When one considers what might have happened if Laughton hadn't informed Olivier that he had made a deal with the Silesian pirates not to take Kirk Douglas and his slave army to Greece, steambath scene fans might be right. The slave revolt would have succeeded, Douglas would have made it to the end of the film and more Greeks would have had clefts in their chins.

House of Strangers (1949). The steambath scene in this rarely shown Joseph L. Manckewicz gem is often used by steambath scene fans to illustrate the restorative powers of steambaths on a wide range of problems. Richard Conte goes there because he's having trouble with his girlfriend, Susan Hayward. His father, Edward G. Robinson, is worried about the authorities looking over "the books." So what's their solution to these problems? More steam.

TELEPHONE

BEST SCENES

Network (1976). Though best known for its window scene ("I'm mad as hell and I'm not going to take it anymore!"), this Sidney Lumet film also contains a nasty telephone scene which must rank as one of the all time great date-breaking moments in screen history. It occurs at the beginning of the William Holden–Faye Dunaway affair. Holden has just asked Dunaway if she's doing anything tonight. Her response is to pick up the telephone, dial a number, and say to whomever it was who answered, "I can't make it tonight, darling. Call you tomorrow." She then hangs up before she gets an answer. Telephone scene fans were so affected by Dunaway's glacial phone manner, they once began to draw up a list of people she may have broken the date with. Some of the names on that list were quite surprising.

Force of Evil (1948). Pound for pound, John Garfield may have been the best telephone scene actor in the business. Revered by telephone scene enthusiasts, he had a special way of expressing fear over the telephone that no actor could duplicate – he licked his lips. The great lip wetting scene in this film is set up by Marie Windsor when she tells Garfield that his phone may be tapped. "If you listen carefully, and try it several times, you can hear a little click," she tells him.

Windsor, who had a thing for Garfield in the movie, rubs it in

157

when she reminds hims that he might spend the rest of his life try-ing to remember what he said over that phone. Later, alone in his office, Garfield picks up the phone to see if it really is tapped. Telephone scene fans in the audience are usually at the edge of their collective seats as Garfield runs his tongue over his lips while holding the phone to his ear. When the "click" is heard, Garfield's eyes grow visibly wider, another nice touch.

But Garfield hasn't exhausted his bag of telephone tricks yet. After he hears the "click," he dials the time. When the time lady tells it to him, Garfield actually starts doing it again, running his tongue over his lips. Telephone scene fans are still debating this one. Was Garfield showing off or was he really afraid of the telephone time lady?

The Birds (1969). In this Hitchcock film portraying bird anger at not being able to use the public telephone, bird scene fans and telephone scene fans have agreed to disagree. Bird scene fans do not think birds are yet capable of dialing a phone and that Tippi Hedren irritated the birds in another way. Telephone scene fans think the birds got mad because Hedren was in that phone booth too long and that birds, like people, have every right to bang on the glass of a public telephone booth when they have an important call to make.

Nothing in Common (1986). Though it was agreed that telephone answering machines should automatically disqualify any telephone scene from consideration in this category, Jackie Gleason's phone call to his son (Tom Hanks) has nevertheless been included. There are two reasons for this exception. First, telephone scene fans always like shots of rooms without people when the phone rings. (Hanks and his girlfriend were in bed and under the covers when Gleason calls.) Second, there were lots of fathers on the panel when this scene was selected. They, more

158

than anyone, would understand the irony of a father having to tell his son's answering machine that his wife of 36 years has left him.

Dial M for Murder (1954). Attracted by the title, telephone scene fans were dismayed when they found themselves watching a movie about someone trying to murder Grace Kelly. At the same time, they were flattered that their favorite instrument was being used to set the murder up, and were able to judge the scene with a fair degree of equanimity. The scene does have a surprisingly high tension level.

First, Ray Milland's watch stops and there is someone using the pay phone at his club so the call that would bring Kelly to the phone to be strangled is late. Then there is the strangler impatiently waiting behind the drape for the call that would bring Kelly to the telephone. Finally, there is the strangling attempt itself, which Milland can hear over his phone, and his surprise and disappointment at finally reaching Kelly and finding her alive. Telephone scene fans agree that while the film itself has become somewhat dated, the telephone scene holds up surprisingly well.

Mildred Pierce (1945). Veda (Ann Blyth) would have known Joan Crawford would never tell the police on her, if she had paid more attention to this award-winning scene, which telephone scene fans like to think of as representing "telephone mother love at its height." When Crawford picks up the phone after Blyth shoots Zachary Scott, even occasional telephone fans know she isn't going to turn her daughter in. They know it from the look Crawford gets on her face when the spoiled Blyth tells her, "It's your fault as well as mine."

If one catches a telephone scene fan at a particularly indiscreet moment, they will admit to knowing a lot of actresses who would have turned Blyth in, especially after they found out that she and Scott had been fooling around behind her back and she had been footing the bill. But not Crawford. No, this is mother love's shining telephone moment and Crawford plays it for all it's worth, winning the votes and admiration of telephone scene fans everywhere.

━━━━━━━━━━━━━━

Telephone scene fans have a particular soft spot for Victor Buono, who in *What Ever Happened to Baby Jane?* couldn't get up the courage to make the call that would get him a job as Bette Davis's accompanist. So he does what any red-blooded American pianist would do. He asks his mother to make the call for him.

Another actor who attracted the notice of telephone scene fans is Chevy Chase. In *Funny Farm* (1988), every time Chase tries to dial a number on his newly installed phone, the operator asks him to deposit 20 cents. The problem is that there is no place to put the coins because the phone is not a pay phone. In an inspired attempt to get his call through, Chase drops two pennies in a glass jar. It doesn't fool the operator, but it did mark him as a telephone scene actor to watch.

TRAIN

BEST SCENES

Strangers on a Train (1951). It's a good thing that train scene fans and train station scene fans are so friendly or the decision about which category the key scene in this film should be placed in might still be in dispute. The problem lies in the opening sequence of scenes which start in a train station but ends up on a train. The camera first picks up a pair of flashy black and white men's shoes. It then cuts to an ordinary pair of men's shoes. Both pairs of shoes seem to be rushing to catch a train, but at no time is the audience allowed to see above the knee.

The four shoes board the train and sit down at the same table. Both pairs of shoes cross their legs and the shoes unintentionally brush one another. The shoes, of course, belong to two of the most popular train scene heroes in recent screen history, Robert Walker and Farley Granger. It is on this train, while having lunch in his compartment, that Walker makes his now famous proposal to Granger, "You do my murder. I do yours."

Of more than marginal interest is the fact that Walker's idea for two stranger's switching murders came just after his idea to make a reservation on the first rocketship to the moon. Officials at NASA were not displeased when Walker did not make it through the film alive. Had he, they might have had a murderer taking mankind's first step on the moon.

A welcome bonus, and one that train station scene fans graciously allowed to be mentioned in this category, is the sight

Robert Walker's now famous proposal to Farley Granger, "You do my murder. I do yours" in *Strangers on a Train* **(1951).**

of Alfred Hitchcock, the film's director, boarding the train carrying a bass fiddle.

Once Upon a Time in the West (1969). Jason Robards is a big favorite of train scene fans if only for his remarkable skill at hanging from a moving train by his feet and still being able to shoot someone in the head through a train window. The scene is set up marvelously. First, we hear Robards's footsteps on the train roof. A gunman follows the footsteps from inside the train. Bronson, tied up in a chair, adds a lot to the excitement with some pretty neat reaction shots. The footsteps stop. There is a tapping on the train window. The gunman turns. Robards's face appears in

162

the train window. Robards smiles at the gunman. Bronson smiles at Robards. Robards aims his gun and shoots the gunman in the head. All in all, a nifty little train scene in a surprisingly good spaghetti western that's played to the hilt by all concerned.

―――――

A Hard Day's Night (1964). This highly eccentric train scene was nearly kept off the ballot because the movie in which it appeared was thought to be a music video. What made it look like a music video was when the Beatles, told not to play their radio by the stuffy Englishman seated in their compartment, are next seen running (and bicycling) beside the train asking if they can have their ball back.

One avid supporter of this particular scene, pointed out that any scene which has a stuffy Englishman saying to the Beatles, "I fought in the war for your sort," and has Ringo responding with, "I'll bet you're sorry you won, then," had to be a real movie. When his line of reasoning did not impress the voting panel, the only three train scene fans old enough to see the film when it originally came out stepped forward and testified that the film did indeed play in movie theatres. It was this evidence that finally cleared the way for this scene to be listed on the ballot, saving it from movie scene oblivion.

―――――

Dollars (1972). A lucky moment for Warren Beatty and a very satisfying one to train scene fans is when Scott Brady drinks a champagne bottle full of undiluted LSD. Brady didn't like it much, though, and has a fit, made all the more horrifying because it takes place in the close quarters of a train compartment. Whatever was in that bottle, it was Brady's realistic thrashing and twitching that won this scene its laurels.

TRAIN STATION

B E S T   S C E N E S

The Dresser (1984). Train station scene fans have always been leery of ham actors when they go near a train station. Their fear is justified by Albert Finney, who, as the actor-manager of a traveling theatrical group, points his walking stick at the departing train he was rushing to catch and shouts in his deepest, most dramatic voice, "Stop...that...train!" In a screech of brakes and a cloud of smoke, the train stops. Train station parapsychologists have so far been unable to explain Finney's unusual effect on trains except to say they will soon be publishing a monograph entitled, *If You Can Intimidate Trains, the World Is Your Oyster.*

Brief Encounter (1945). Not many film fans are aware of it, but the main sitting room of the train station fan club is an exact reproduction of the train station tea shop where Celia Johnson and Trevor Howard carried on most of their extramarital affair. Before entering this room, visitors are required to bathe their left eye in a glass of water, just as Celia Johnson did when she got that cinder in her eye. This ritual, of course, recreates the scene in which Johnson meets Howard, the doctor who removes the cinder and falls in love with her.

Train station scene fans are still amazed at how Johnson managed to bathe her eye with an ordinary glass of water without

165

FLAMES OF PASSION

A rare shot of Celia Johnson and Trevor Howard away from the train station tea shop in *Brief Encounter* (1945).

spilling one drop on her dress. One theory is that it was not an ordinary glass, but an eye cup that was kept in the tea shop especially for passengers who were prone to cinders. All of which opens up the possibility of other train station affairs beginning in the same way, affairs that Noel Coward chose not to write about. But all that is another kettle of tea. The movie is enormously popular with train station fans worldwide. Their favorite line in the film? When Celia Johnson, concerned that Trevor Howard will miss his train, says to him, "Don't bother about me. My train's not due for two minutes."

In the Heat of the Night (1967). When Rod Steiger, who plays a small town sheriff, says to Sidney Poitier, who plays a big-city detective, "Virgil, you take care, you hear," in the last scene of the film, we know why train station scene fans suspended the "100-foot rule" and voted this scene its just award. Steiger's words are so full of unspoken feeling and Poitier's farewell smile so full of tenderness that the fact the railroad station measured less than the required 100 feet (as is stated in the train station fan club bylaws) was quietly overlooked.

Summertime (1955). Scratch a train station scene fan and you'll often find a romantic. When Rossano Brazzi runs along the station platform after Katharine Hepburn's train carrying that box of white gladiolas, they are all rooting for him. So, Brazzi didn't quite manage to catch the train, but he does open the box to show her that they are white gladiolas. These are the same flowers she lost in the canal.

When Hepburn sees them, she at least knows that he loves her. Train station fans not so romantically inclined point out that if this weren't Venice, Brazzi would have been in better shape (one can't jog each morning on the Grand Canal) and might have even caught up with Hepburn's train. Then he could have given her the flowers and she could have taken them back with her to the States.

———————————

Love in the Afternoon (1957). In Venice, it's the men who bring flowers to women at train stations that they never give them (Rossano Brazzi to Katharine Hepburn in *Summertime*); in Paris, that is reversed. It's the women who bring flowers to men in train stations that they never give them. Yes, the flowers Audrey Hepburn is holding are for Gary Cooper, but she never gives them to him. To get them, Cooper has to swoop Hepburn onto the train and take her back to America with him. Train station scene fans always considered Brazzi unlucky because he never got within Katharine Hepburn's swooping range.

———————————

*Mr Hulot's Holiday (1935). The very funny train station scene at the beginning of this film would have won its award without being asterisked had train station scene fans not invoked their exclusivity rule. It states that no train station scene can be given an award if other scenes in the film have already received one. Since this Tati film already had both a cemetery and a bird scene award when the voting took place, it could only be relegated to this footnote. The scene in question, of course, is charming; one in which a group of tourists, listening to the announcement on what track their train will leave from, are continually made to shuffle from one platform to the next. Naturally, when the train finally arrives, they are on the wrong one.

WHISTLING

B E S T   S C E N E S

To Have and Have Not (1944). It was Rule 6 that finally cleared the way for this whistling cult favorite. Rule 6 in the Whistling Scene Manual (Revised Edition) states: "A whistling scene need not contain an actual whistle if either an oral or written description of a whistle is given." Any whistling scene fan worth his or her wind could be woken up in the middle of the night, hung by his or her toes and still be able to recite Lauren Bacall's unforgettable exit line to Humphrey Bogart, "You know how to whistle, don't you? You just put your lips together and blow."

The High and the Mighty (1954). In that unforgettable final scene when John Wayne walks away from the plane after having kept it from crash-landing into the ocean, the whistled tune played in the soundtrack had an effect on film fans which lasted long after they left the movie theatre. Whistling scene fans report that all during the year the film was released, they would hear that tune whistled by motorists running out of gas, by spouses returning home without a birthday present, even by passersby on the way to the dentist.

They argue, and rightly so, that no whistling scene which had become such a widespread symbol for courage in the face of adversity, could ever be denied its place in film history. If this wasn't reason enough for its selection, whistling scene fans point out this was the movie which gave Robert Stack the courage he needed to try out for his role in *Airplane* (1980).

———————

The Bridge on the River Kwai (1957). What inspired Alec Guinness's regiment to begin whistling the "Colonel Bogie March" as they marched into that Japanese prisoner of war camp is still a question being pondered by whistling scene fans. Nevertheless, the effect is quite remarkable. So good were they that when the men appear to be whistled out, a full marching band joins them on the soundtrack. Even Sessue Hayakawa, the camp commander, was impressed.

David Lean, the director of this film about the positive effects of whistling on POWs, thought it was so good that he made it the opening scene. John Hughes, director of *The Breakfast Club* (1985), liked it so much he used it again in his film about troubled teenagers. In Hughes's whistling scene, one of the boys in detention class starts whistling the same "Colonel Bogie March." The other teenagers join him until they are all whistling it. Then a band on the soundtrack joins in, until marching music fills the classroom.

Though it is certainly a whistling scene of award caliber (that they are sitting down while whistling a march is an especially nice touch), it couldn't be considered for a whistling scene award. Whistling scene rules clearly state: "When a whistling scene is duplicated in another film, it is the whistling scene in the earlier film that shall be deemed eligible for the award." Since *The Bridge on the River Kwai* was made nearly 30 years earlier than *The Breakfast Club*, the later film can be nothing more than an interesting whistling sidelight.

———————

Snow White and the Seven Dwarfs (1937). Whistling scene fans as a group are certainly not afraid to take risks. They

170

include not one but two animated features on their list. In the first, which also happened to be Walt Disney's first full-length feature production, the whistling is done at work to a song most movie fans still remember, "Whistle While You Work." This selection, however, was the cause of some disharmony among male and female members of the judging panel. The dwarfs (Dopey, Grumpy, Sleepy, Sneezy, Doc, Happy, and Bashful) whistle while they work in their diamond mine. Snow White whistles while she cleans up their cottage. The matter was resolved when it was agreed that the film was made at a time when male and female roles were less overlapping.

Pinocchio (1940). In this second animated feature to be listed, whistling scene fans like to point out the importance of whistling scenes in teaching a moral lesson. When Jiminy Cricket starts to sing, "Take the straight and narrow path, and if you start to slide, give a little whistle, and always let your conscience be your guide," whistling fans take this message to heart. You can usually spot whistling scene fans in the audience. Whenever Pinocchio starts doing dumb things, they are whistling. It's something Pinocchio should have been doing when he meets Stromboli. If he had, he never would have grown those donkey ears.

"M" (1931). Whistling scene paparazzi still insist that Peter Lorre whistled in this Fritz Lang classic because he was nervous about it being his first film. This notion was quashed once and forever by whistling scene historians who report that the whistling was definitely in the script. The only way the blind balloon vendor could discover the identity of the child murderer was to recognize the tune Lorre whistled when he bought balloons for the children he planned to murder.

An interesting footnote is that the tune Lorre was originally supposed to have whistled was Strauss's *Tales from the Vienna Woods*. Unfortunately, soon after the film began shooting it was discovered that the only tune the blind balloon vendor could recognize was the first few bars to, "In the Hall of the Mountain King," from Grieg's *Peer Gynt*. Lorre was not so familiar with this tune, which explains why so much of his whistling is off key.

It should also be noted that balloon scene enthusiasts have had a long-standing claim to this scene. However, it was judged that since the whistling element was more important to the film than the balloon element, the scene should be placed in the whistling category. Since whistling scene fans do not allow their scenes to be considered for other category awards, here it remains.

The Man Who Knew Too Much (1956). The importance of whistling is the moral of this overlong Alfred Hitchcock tale about international spies. If Daniel Gelin, the young actor who played Doris Day's son, Hank, had not known how to whistle "Qué Sera, Sera," Jimmy Stewart would never have known what room he was kept prisoner in nor would he have been able to rescue him from the kidnappers. Whistling scene fans also like to think that Gelin's whistling ability was partly responsible for the song's winning an Oscar that year.

The King and I (1956). Deborah Kerr surprised whistling scene fans with a pretty snappy rendition of "Whistle a Happy Tune," to ease her son's fears about meeting the King of Siam. (Whistling as a cure for apprehension has always counted a lot with whistling scene fans.) By the time Kerr begins to sing, "While shivering in my shoes, I strike a careless pose, and whistle a happy tune, so nobody knows I'm afraid," to her son and her son begins to feel better about meeting Yul Brynner, whistling scene fans were completely won over. That her voice was dubbed by Marni Nixon was never concealed by Kerr and had no effect on the voting since her whistle was real. As it says in the song, "For when I fool the people I fear, I fool myself as well."

———————————

Among the many actors who made the most of their whistling scenes, two stand out. Leslie Howard, whistling "Oh, there's a tavern in the town," as he steps into the fog and across the Swiss border in *Pimpernel Smith* (1941) and Christopher Plummer, who as Captain Von Trapp in *The Sound of Music* (1965) made up for his lack of whistling ability by using a bosun's whistle to call his children.

WINDOW

B E S T   S C E N E S

Chariots of Fire (1981). No window scene has ever generated as much emotion as the one in which Ian Holm looks out of his Paris hotel window and sees the British flag being raised above the Olympic stadium to the strains of "God Save the Queen." To Holm, who plays Ben Cross's track coach, it meant that Cross had won the race and the gold medal. Window scene fans feel that because this shot was framed through the narrow confines of a hotel window the emotional impact of the scene was greatly heightened.

Holm, an actor who certainly knows how to look out of a window, was so overcome by emotion he had to sit down. In an effort to publicize what a good window scene can do for a movie, window scene fans have sent clips of this scene to producers and directors of every movie-making nation. The results of this public relations effort are not yet conclusive.

Beverly Hills Cop (1984). There are only two possible window shots. In window scene jargon they are called, "innies" and "outies." An "innie" is when the camera is inside and looking out. An "outie" is when the camera is outside looking in. On rare occasions, a window scene comes along that is both an "innie" and an "outie." It usually causes quite a stir among fans of this genre. This is precisely what occurred when Eddie Murphy gets thrown out of that plate glass window in Beverly Hills. The camera was outside looking in and Murphy was inside being thrown out. When Murphy gets arrested for being thrown out of the window it becomes rarer still: a window scene that is also quite funny.

———

The Bad and the Beautiful (1952). One of the strangest window scenes ever to come out of Hollywood takes place in a car. When Lana Turner discovers that Kirk Douglas doesn't love her anymore she rushes out of his mansion and drives off in her car. When Turner sees drops on the window, she turns on the window wipers. But it isn't raining and they are not raindrops. She's crying and what she thought were raindrops were really tears. Back when this film was made, this was considered a pretty nifty scene. Today, it seems rather silly. Not to window fans though.

———

Rear Window (1954). Though seasoned window scene fans certainly appreciate the multiplicity of window scenes that Jimmy Stewart is privy to in this movie – Judith Evelyn (Miss Lonely Hearts) having dinner with her imaginary suitor; the dog being lowered down to the courtyard each day; the dog's murder; the beautiful but fickle dancer and her suitors; the sensitive composer, the newlyweds, and of course, Raymond Burr, his complaining wife and the suspicious goings-on in that apartment, it is the marvelous sequence of dénouements to these window vignettes that they find most pleasing.

Miss Lonely Hearts finally meets the composer, the dead dog's owners get a new dog, the fickle dancer's runty boyfriend returns from the army, the honeymoon couple start bickering, Burr gets caught, Stewart breaks his other leg falling out of the window, and most important of all, Burr's old apartment becomes vacant. In a city where good apartments are so hard to find, that is something worth murdering for.

A marvelous sequence of window vignettes in *Rear Window* (1954).

The Day of the Jackal (1973). A window scene that is both funny and frightening occurs near the end of this Frederick Forsythe adaptation about a plot to assassinate Charles de Gaulle. Crouching at a window overlooking the Tomb of the Unknown Soldier, Edward Fox has de Gaulle in the sights of his homemade rifle. The French general has just stopped in front of a very short dignitary. At the instant Fox fires, de Gaulle bends down to shake the near midget's hand. As a result of this politeness, the bullet flies harmlessly over his head. Had the dignitary he was shaking hands with been anywhere near normal height, de Gaulle would have been successfully assassinated.

Raising Arizona (1987). A very funny window scene, quite unique, in fact, was inserted into this sometimes funny movie about a couple who kidnap a baby quintuplet. It's shot from the baby's POV, which is screenwriter talk for "point of view," and it works. The baby is facing the window and looking at Nicolas Cage, who is on a ladder looking in. Because the baby is being bounced by her nanny, the camera bounces, too. The result of all this is that we see Cage moving up and down as he would be seen by the baby he is about to kidnap. Window scene fans love this kind of stuff and gave it their highest rating.

Network (1976). The bimonthly meetings of the window scene fan club are always open and I happened to attend the one in which this satire on window use was selected. Though the winning scene's lustre has been slightly diminished by time, window scene fans are still thrilled when they see windows all across the nation opening and people popping their heads out and yelling, "I'm mad as hell and I'm not going to take it anymore!"

This is the first time such an orchestrated chorus of window yells have ever appeared on screen and it certainly deserved its award.

INDEX

B E S T　　S C E N E S